Eating with History

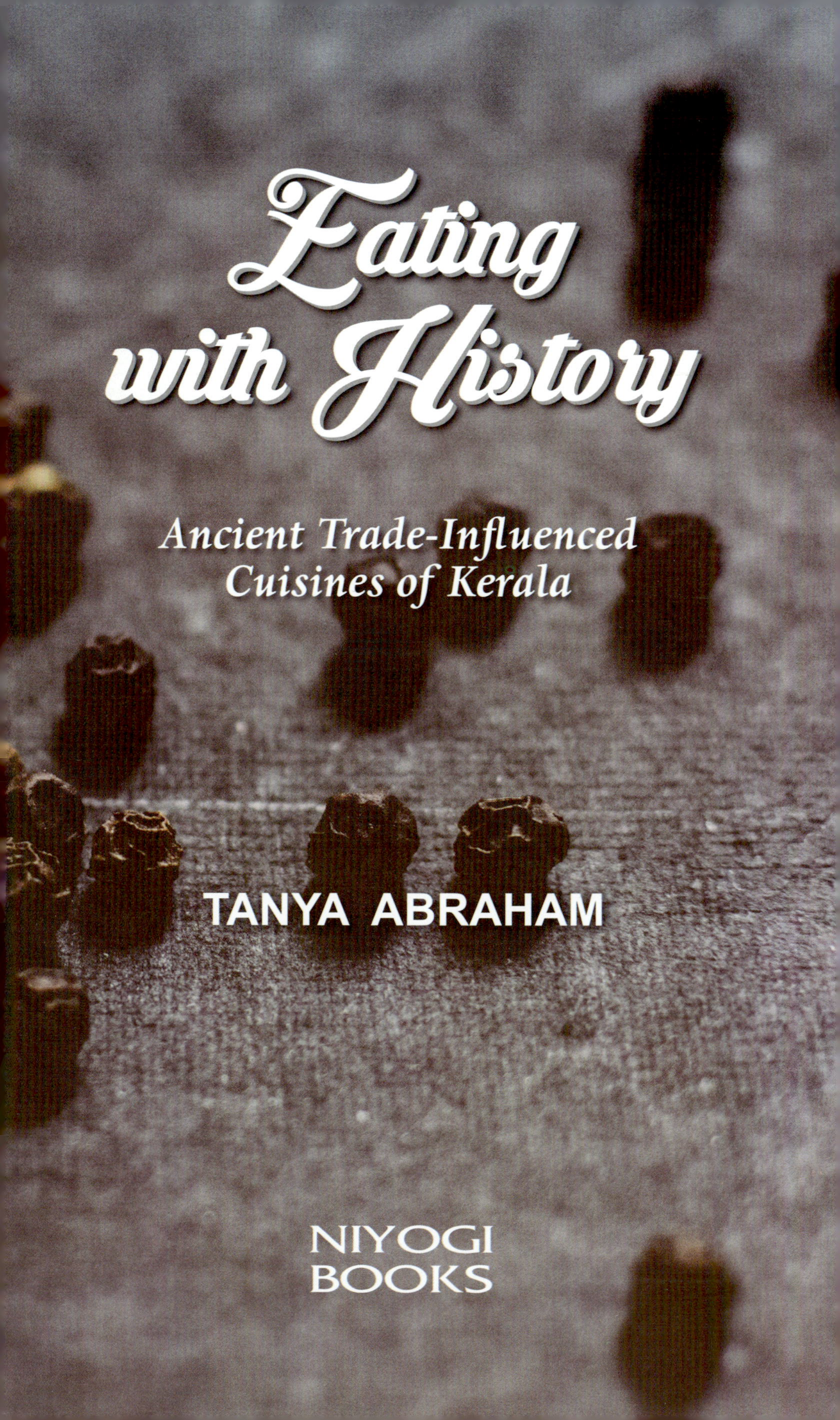

Eating with History

Ancient Trade-Influenced Cuisines of Kerala

TANYA ABRAHAM

NIYOGI
BOOKS

Published by
NIYOGI BOOKS
Block D, Building No. 77
Okhla Industrial Area, Phase-I
New Delhi-110 020, INDIA
Tel: 91-11-26816301, 26818960
Email: niyogibooks@gmail.com
Website: www.niyogibooksindia.com

Editor: Mohua Mitra
Design: Nabanita Das
Cover Design: Author

ISBN: 978-93-89136-26-5
Publication: 2020
First reprint: 2022

Printed at: Niyogi Offset Pvt. Ltd., New Delhi, India

Domestic fishing boats in Kochi now dock where once anchored large canoes that carried spices for trade

Pg 2-3: Whole black pepper, widely grown in Kerala, is an important ingredient in the region's ethnic cuisine

In memory of my grandmother,
Annie Burleigh Kurishingal.

To my mother, for soul food

To keep the home alive, at its core, remained my grandmother's kitchen. Homemade rose cookies were an integral part of the traditional food produced in this kitchen

CONTENTS

The food trail is extensive. There are numerous recipes in each community in Kerala. These communities, influenced by foreign trade, drew their uniqueness from the marrying of flavours through cultures. Bazaar Road in Mattancherry, the Jew Town, housed godowns for spice trade.Many of the ancient buildings and communities still exist

FOREWORD

It gives me immense pleasure to write a few words on Tanya Abraham's *Eating with History: Ancient Trade-Influenced Cuisines of Kerala*. This book is an invaluable compendium of a variety of food recipes that evolved out of Kerala's kitchen, thanks to the creative and nuanced cross-cultural interactions that happened through the channels of trade. By analysing the historical contexts within which different communities (like the Jews, Syrian Christians, Muslims, Anglo-Indians etc.,) and their consumption culture appeared in Kerala, Tanya Abraham has provided scholars with new ways of understanding the unique but varied and rich food culture of Kerala. The initial part of the work–historically contextualising the webs of cultural connectivities of Kerala–provides a useful introduction to the understanding of the ways how its various threads of culinary culture got evolved and got mixed with various elements of foreign food culture, always creating new textures, tastes and flavours in the process of local adaptations. The range of the book is of such sweep and vastness that it conveys a nuanced and layered understanding of the wide variety of historical processes with which different parallel food traditions evolved among Christians, Jews, Muslims and Anglo-Indians, evidently suggesting a certain amount of exclusiveness among them on food matters despite sharing the same space and same living conditions. The author shows that it happens mainly because of the creative meanings that each community gives to the food ingredients, which eventually is made to evolve as its marker of identity. The recipes of most of the food items of various communities of Kerala are also given in meticulous detail, which in

Meen pollichathu cooked with the fresh catch of the day in Syrian Christian style, exudes one of the many unique flavours of Kerala

turn serve as a rich guide for every household to prepare and taste the best food of the land. I am delighted to say that this easy-to-read book is valuable and well written, with a refreshing sense of excitement at the vast range of knowledge packed in the recipes of every kind of regional food and dish that Kerala is famous for. It is a valuable treasure for the students and researchers of Indian food culture and an easy reference book for every household that treasures and wants to prepare and taste the best food from the past. As there is no authentic work so far on the historical contextualisation of the eating traditions of various communities of Kerala and their recipes, this is a long overdue publication. I eagerly look forward to its publication and subsequent availability in the larger world of food lovers, academicians, and readers keen to learn the history and the process of cultural evolution in Kerala.

Dr Pius Malekandathil
Professor
Centre for Historical Studies, Jawaharlal Nehru University, New Delhi

PREFACE

This book is in honour of the creativity and work of the many women in kitchens across Kerala, for cherishing the recipes passed down generations and bringing heart to homes. In my three years of study, it was understood that these communities, influenced by foreign trade in Kerala, drew their uniqueness from the marrying of flavours through cultures. It is assumed that in an otherwise predominantly vegetarian region, a variety of meats, fish and other seafood rose to become dominant foods at a later stage, curried to life from outside influences. The food trail is extensive, and I believe I may have only skimmed the surface of the food trove of these communities. There are numerous recipes in each community, each conjured up by women in families across Kerala; it was not however possible to document all of them. Yet, the journey has been rewarding in multifarious ways: to all those who spent time with me explaining the nuances of their kitchen fare, all the while collecting recipes from relatives and friends, and for the hospitality that brought to the conversations flavours new, thank you.

Between stone jars of pickles, the smell of firewood and burning coal...stood my grandmother

AMMAMA'S KUSINCHYA

I grew up in a small town in Kerala, in a big *tarawad*[1] that housed not only our large family but also the town happenings. It was a wondrous home, which has, for generations, been the backbone of our family; like a melting pot of various condiments that provided a variety of flavours to those who lived in it. There was politics and the freedom movement. There were rooms, which housed nationalists and businessmen, foreign visitors and missionaries. It remained an open house, with a family, which decreased in size as members left for business or higher education, and increased as distant relatives visited and stayed for months. There were so many people at a given time that it never seemed a home to one single family alone. Instead it housed an eclectic energy that came from the lives of the many who walked in and out its doors. To keep the home alive, at its core, remained my grandmother's kitchen. We called it *kusinchya*[2], a Portuguese derivative of the word 'kitchen', and it was from ammama's[3] *kusinchya* that the main artery ran to nourish the soul of the household. Between stone jars of pickles, the smell of firewood and burning coal, and the chatter of servants stood my grandmother in her customary *chatta* and *mundu*[4], the traditional attire prescribed to Kerala Catholic women. What started as virgin white every morning yellowed as the hours in the kitchen clocked by, the smell of masala clinging generously to the cotton of her clothing. There was so much cooking all at once that it was strange that never was a recipe book ever visible with her, except a copy of the first edition of Mrs Beaton's cookbook, gifted to her by an English acquaintance, which was once in a

Lawns were decorated with fairy lights during parties. A shamiana was set up in the backyard to serve as the temporary kitchen of the Kurishingal tarawad

while read through. And she never followed anyone's cooking instructions either. She had an uncanny knack of producing flavours even before the pot was on the fire. Throwing in ingredients from her well-stocked kitchen, everyday saw an exciting array of dishes at the *unnumuri*[5], the dining room that sat on either side of the courtyard of the two-hundred-and-fifty-year-old house. I used to often wonder if her entourage of servants was ever a sufficient hand to support her in fulfilling the needs of the family. Whilst one wanted a fiery fish curry with rice for lunch, the other preferred pork and chicken, with vegetables to accompany. Her husband and the head of the household, my grandfather whom I fondly remember, had a simple palate who preferred dishes less spiced, and was often satisfied with a bowl of clear soup or *kanji* and fish roe curry. Between him, her unmarried brothers-in-law, four sons, their wives and a battalion of grand-children, Mrs Annie Burleigh, as she was known outside the family, had a grand task to fulfill every day. Whenever I stopped by the *kusinchya* to satisfy my curious young mind, she would, over a steaming vessel, narrate stories of how as a young bride she cooked for my great-grandfather (her

Over steaming vessels, grandmother narrated stories of how as a young bride she cooked for my great-grandfather—her father-in-law

father-in-law) whom she revered greatly, a stalling figure in town during British reign. And how recipes for sandwiches and pies were conjured up as foreign visitors met with him at the *tarawad* gardens. When few Keralites used handcrafted wooden trays with lace tray cloth, she had them specially made to display culinary culture. She trained her kin to be courteous and relish foods from other lands, which were first introduced from the ships that docked at Cochin Harbour. Later, she would make her own version of corned beef and smoked ham, which began to be customarily served with a punch made from local arrack. On her travels she would bring home with her recipes that would soon be the highlight of an evening family gathering. Ammama had an uncanny knack to accentuate anything and everything to do with food—she never for once allowed recipes or ideas slip away. Instead, she would build upon them and present them in a manner, which brought her much applaud and praise. To make eating an occasion, she often reminded us of the importance of wise dining. It was she who taught me to use cutlery and chew my food slowly to allow the flavours to coat my tongue. Her skills never cease[d] to amaze me, like when she formed cutlets

Drawing of the Kurishingal Tarawad, year 2012, by artist and a member of the household, Priti Vadakkath

with one palm, throwing them in hot fat in a continuous rhythm whilst stirring curry with the other, simultaneously monitoring the cooking for at least forty people at any given time.

When Christmas drew near, everything changed in the *kusinchya*, including the ingredients on the shelves. Pork was salted, fresh fruit preserved in sugar syrup. Halwa, cakes, and wines from varied fruits were churned out incessantly, wrapped in decorative paper and sent cycling to neighbouring homes. These were homes, which used to send us gifts of festivity, during Jewish festivals or Bakr-id, for example. Fort Cochin's wondrous amalgamation of cultures brought to our doorstep foods from various backgrounds, recipes of generations that were prepared by the ladies of households. Each one stood evidently different from the other, as flavours shifted dramatically, and their arrival was always looked forward to in great earnest. Two days after the grand family Christmas celebration at

home, the family opened its doors to guests for its eagerly looked forward to Christmas party. The lawns were decorated in white and blue lights, crockery hired and bearers wore starched white uniforms. The *kusinchya* that day always took upon a new look. A shamiana spread across its backyard near the pond, and cooking was shifted to the temporary open-air kitchen. A *kokie*[6] was hired, who in advance had to produce a list of his best dishes to my grandmother. On close scrutiny, she would strike off those, which did not appeal to her palate and spruce them up with her own concoctions. The dining tables would then be filled with the most delicious fare, from suckling pig and leg of ham to more traditional Latin Catholic curries. When ice cream was a rarity, Ammama had them churned out by hand, like her popular vanilla spiced with orange-rind. This, she filled in orange and placed them over a brass urn of crushed ice. As interesting as it seemed then, the feat of filling 200 cases today baffles me as I look back at her in awe. Her Christmas parties were always the talk of the town. And although the children of the house were never allowed to attend them, we were fortunate to be party to the cooking frenzy that went on in the backyard. The sound of sizzling oil, the warmth of steaming rice and the stickiness of sugar syrup on the wooden tables still seem so real. The anxious voice of the *kokie* giving orders still echoes in my ear against the chatter from the lawns. The glimpses of silk saris and shiny boots were always fascinating to my young mind. But they fade away when compared to the soothing comfort that was found under the kitchen shamiana.

When Ammama passed on at the age of 104, a storehouse of culinary delights went with her. Yet everyday, to date, her curries are recalled with deep love. So many years later, I can still see her next to the wood-stove, and smell the flavours in the air. It made me think of all the women like her, who ran households and brought to life recipes passed down generations in their kitchens. It is a reason why this book has been penned—Kerala is a fascinating land of great history and culture; the foods from its kitchen stand witness to generations of adventure, which continue to stand as testimony to the land's rich history.

Annie Burleigh was not only a culinary expert, but also a freedom fighter, founder of the Mahila Samajam in Kerala and a municipal councillor (of the governing body in Fort Cochin) for fifteen years. Whilst the men of the household dedicated themselves to business and Indian Independence, she preserved the Kurishingal household, the base for the freedom movement in Cochin for more than half a century, keeping it nourished day after day.

Endnotes

1. *Tarawad – Family house*
2. *Kusinchya – Derived from Portuguese, the word means 'kitchen' and was used in regions influenced by Portuguese rule*
3. *Ammama – Malayalam for 'grandmother'*
4. *Chatta and mundu –Traditional attire worn by Kerala Catholic women*
5. *Unnumuri – Dining room*
6. *Kokie – Cook, a derivative from Portuguese*

KERALA AND FOOD

In the heart of Kerala, lies the love of its people for food. As cultures and traditions thrived in the state, food found a prominent position in people's lives. Influenced greatly by traditions, religious beliefs and trade, it led to the emergence of a variety of cuisines. In kitchens brewed recipes that came from innovative ideas and new ingredients, marrying to form exclusive and distinct flavours. These flavours changed from one community to another, even from one household to another. Food entwined itself intricately to people's lives and became an inextricable part of living.

Kerala's history is soaked in stories of cultural diversity and a heritage that has created an identity unique to it. The story goes that when Lord Parasuram, one of the ten avatars of Lord Vishnu, threw his axe into the Arabian Sea, he fetched out a piece of land that bore great beauty and wealth. And thus, the story of spices began, found in the verdant, tropical forests of Kerala. News of this rich land spread across the oceans, and ships plied their way to its shores in search of wealth. With the arrival of new cultures, emerged new communities, which created a blend of peoples unique to Kerala alone. A significant part of this cultural emergence was the birth of various cuisines, developed as a consequence of religion, rituals, foreign food ingredients, and the adaption of local food to favour new palates. The marrying of communal traditions meant the coming together of new practices, of which food remained a significant explanatory of identities that made a community unique. The recipe books of yore that have preserved food that emerged from foreign influences, trace their

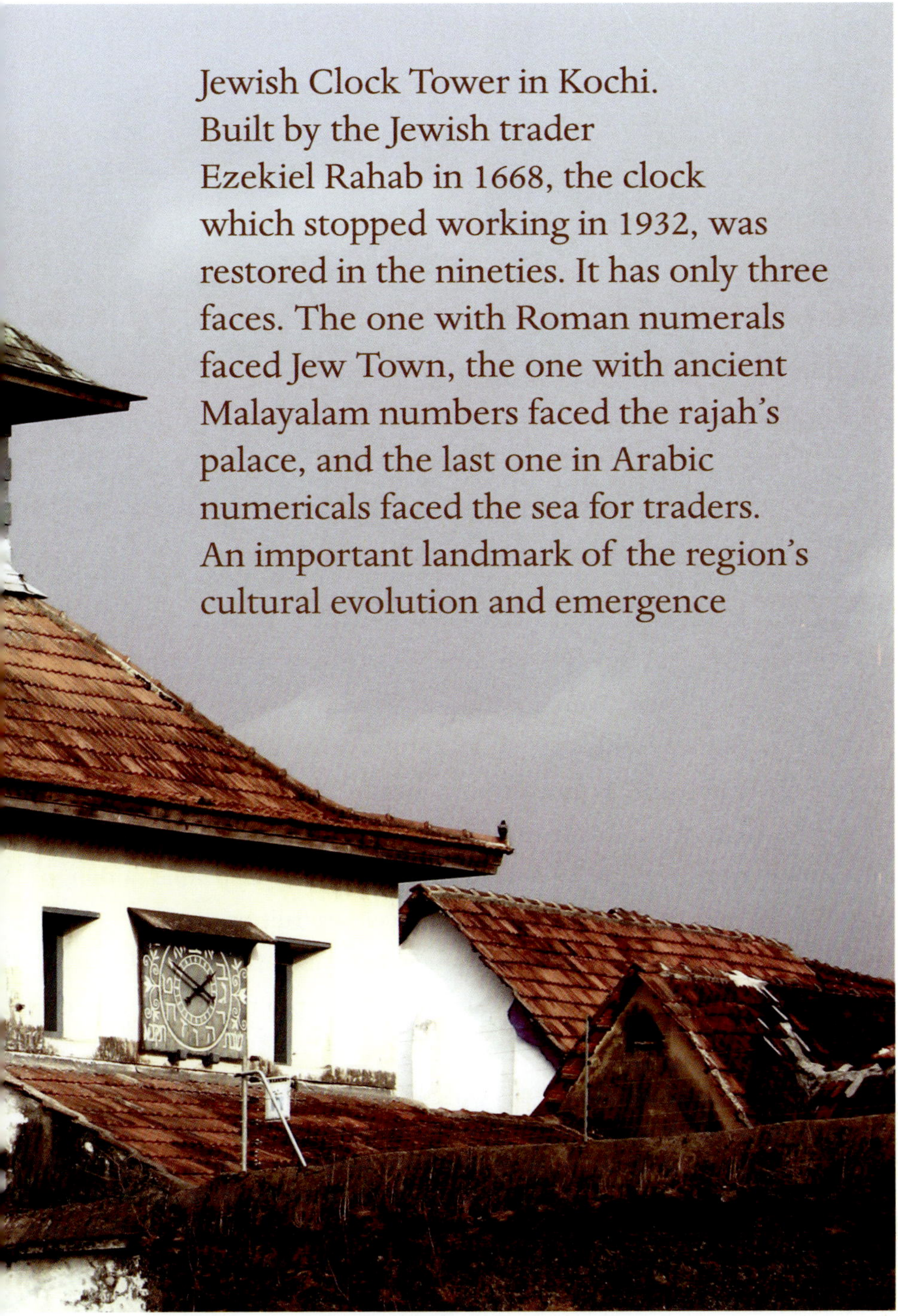

Jewish Clock Tower in Kochi.
Built by the Jewish trader
Ezekiel Rahab in 1668, the clock
which stopped working in 1932, was
restored in the nineties. It has only three
faces. The one with Roman numerals
faced Jew Town, the one with ancient
Malayalam numbers faced the rajah's
palace, and the last one in Arabic
numericals faced the sea for traders.
An important landmark of the region's
cultural evolution and emergence

Left to right: *Paradesi Jewish women on the narrow streets of Jew Town in Mattancherry in the evenings enjoy a game of cards and conversation; a community congregation of Malabari Jews within the premises of their synagogue. One among the many beliefs regarding the arrival of the Jews is of their presence in the 10th century* BC, *King Solomon's times*

emergence to the spice trade; the ancient seaport of Muziris and regions of the Malabar, which lured ships to its shores in search of black pepper. Tamil literature refers to *yavanas* (foreign ships, from Rome and Egypt) arriving with gold and perfumes and returning with pepper.[1]

Pliny the Elder, a Roman writer (AD 23-79), writes, 'It is quite surprising that the use of pepper has come so much into fashion, seeing that for other substances which we use, it is sometimes their sweetness and sometimes their appearance that has attracted our notice; whereas, pepper has nothing in it that can plead as a recommendation to either fruit or berry, it's only desirable quality being a certain pungency; and yet it is for this that we import it all the way from India!'[2] Pliny was the first to make trial of it as an article of food.

With trade came new religions, new identities and new ways of living. The reason for the unique flourishing of communities for centuries owes its gratitude to the rulers of the time who welcomed foreign settlements, for the main reason of economic gain. Seen as highly tolerant and secular in thought, the ruling kings offered land and permission to new nationalities to establish their communities, including permission to marry local women and raise families. This open acceptance of foreign cultures saw the rise of new communities, and the growth of a society that flourished as a mélange of these. The cultural identities, which developed through foreign contact, in spite of the tolerant climate that prevailed, held tightly to identities in the form of rituals, religious practices, and specific food habits (specific kinds of food remained closely attached to specific cultures, the adulteration of which was minimal). It is important to understand that, for the evolution of these new cuisines, there was an interesting development of food associations such as food laws and ingredients used by distinct sections of people, in distinct manners.

Civilisations to Conquerors— Cooking and Eating Patterns

In India, we see that during the Indus Valley Civilisation–the oldest civilisation (4500 BCE)–came the cultivation of eggplant and sesame. Consequently, by 3000 BCE, other agricultural produce like turmeric, cardamom, black pepper and mustard were grown. Agriculture, thus, developed gradually, and with it the blending of ingredients, which gave rise to new flavours and cooking styles. But during the Vedic times and with the advent of Ayurveda, fruits and vegetables, along with non-processed sweeteners like honey became the main products of consumption. Later, with the propagation of foods for healthy living, the preaching of ahimsa in Buddhism and the belief in karma by Hindus, (which induced them not to harm other living organisms), led India to remain largely a vegetarian state for a long period of time. Keralites too, like

A firewood kitchen, when large scale cooking in joint families of traditional houses called a tarawad was an everyday feature. Puttu is being steamed in a puttu maker, for breakfast

the rest of India had learnt to adapt to the produce of the land, depending heavily on agriculture and the forests. It was the influence from conquerors afar that drastically changed eating patterns and influenced cooking in myriad ways.

In central and northern India, with the arrival of conquerors from Persia, Arabia and the like, a whole new cooking technology with new ingredients were introduced. Food became elaborate, with rich dishes and the introduction of apricots, plums and pista in cooking, for example. Along with it, came meat as a strong food item, so much that we see the mutton biryani as a famous dish that has encouraged many variants all through the country. And then there is coffee, first brought by the Arabs, which was transformed into a sweet version with milk and sugar. However, if we view Kerala separately, we see that the infiltration of these influences from northern and central India were slow, for Kerala remained a secluded country owing to the Western Ghats, the sea offering the only easy accessibility to the land. And so, the largest influences came from the rulers of foreign origin who had settlements in ancient port towns. They stayed for extensive periods of time, sometimes centuries, which led to the open mingling with natives and native ingredients. Thus came about a whole new variety of foods. The spice trade, undoubtedly, was the start to this great food adventure. The spices from the Malabar hills of Kerala were shipped to Arabia, from where they were carried to lands such as Mesopotamia and Egypt. These spices, thus, were not only the foundation of cooking in India, but became the essential ingredients in many other cuisines as well.

Christianity and Catholicism—Arrival of the Portuguese

The enormous demand for spices, especially black pepper, brought a train of conquerors to Kerala. Like the Portuguese, for example, who came to Kerala in the 15th century and brought with them potatoes, chillies, tomato, cashew nut, guava, papaya and pineapple (they introduced 300 plants in

India). And in Kerala, they improved the cultivation of spices like ginger, pepper, cardamom and cinnamon, which had great demand in Europe.(**II**)[3] Explorers of great vision, the Portuguese were widely connected the world over—from Brazil to Malacca in Malaysia, so it was only obvious that they brought numerous products and recipes into India from various countries they conquered. Fruit like custard apple, which is often mistaken to have been of Indian origin, was brought by the Portuguese from South America. The citrus fruit *mosambi* of the orange family, was brought from Mozambique, and thus, the name. The fruit was greatly revered by Portuguese seafarers on learning that eating it cured dying sailors of a strange disease. Its high content of vitamin C protected them against scurvy, an illness that they encountered on voyages, for which no cure was found but from the fruit of the trees found in Mozambique.

It must also be understood that the Portuguese deeply integrated with the locals in Kerala, although their direct influence can be witnessed very minimally today in comparison to Goa (largely owing to the recentness of their presence in Goa and the European powers who arrived in Kerala later). The Anglo-Indian community (**III**) in Fort Cochin and Thangassery in Quilon (Kollam) for example, still preserve details of their presence in recipes passed through the generations. Records with the Catholic Church in Kerala clearly state that the Portuguese married natives, 'establishing a specific community that looked and spoke differently.'[4] Dr Sergio Mascarenhas in his work titled *Christians and Cochin: The Religious Factor in the Portuguese Establishment of Cochin*, explains of a policy that was introduced in AD 1510, encouraging alliances between Portuguese men and native women. Mix of cultures meant a mix of cuisines as well, where local spices blend with flavours from Portugal. Like, *pigadosi* (a sweetened porridge of boiled plantains and coconut milk) or the famous *vindhaloo* (vindaloo), which is a native derivative of pork preserve the Portuguese used to cook in red wine, vinegar and garlic. Very often Portuguese recipes were combined with locally available ingredients like coconut, for

The trail showing the ancient Spice Route

THE ICE SEA
indian sea

An Anglo-Indian wedding in the 1970s. This Christian community in Kerala followed western culture in their dress and habits, to a large extent

example, which resulted in a whole new range of dishes that Kerala, at the time, was unaccustomed to.

Of the many food ingredients introduced by the Portuguese, it is vinegar, which was a prime influencer of Kerala cuisine. Although India was producing vinegar prior to Portuguese arrival, it was they who introduced it in cooking. The Portuguese used vinegar extensively in their food; especially to preserve salted meats with paprika and garlic which were stored in large barrels during their voyages in ships to lands afar. This proved to be a quick savouring dish when fried in oil, close to the meat pickle famously relished in Kerala today. The red chilli peppers are yet another introduction, which changed cooking greatly. Fish and meat curries took upon a whole new flavour with red chilli peppers used dry or fresh, whole or ground. Also, importantly, they brought yeast into the country and provided locals with leavened bread, previously unknown in Kerala. Since ovens were not used at the time, the Portuguese, to make breads, steamed or roasted flattened rice dough in earthen vessels. Thus, emerged a version of the original *bolo* eaten in Portugal even today (which is also called *bolo* in Kerala, a Portuguese bread still made in homes of regions of Portuguese influence, of rice-flour and coconut). However, their love for freshly baked cakes and bread lured them to create native firewood ovens known as the *borma*. Streets in Fort Cochin had numerous bakeries, where bread was baked daily. Some of the recipes continue to this day, providing a special, homemade feel to these breads.

It was not only food that underwent change. Eating habits became more refined as well. Natives who ate off the banana leaf began using utensils of porcelain, and sat themselves on tables and chairs in specific dining areas than being seated on kitchen floors. Exquisite Chinese porcelain came to Kerala on ships that sailed through the spice route. Also utensils like the Chinese wok called *cheenachati* and Chinese urns that were filled with honey and shipped to the Kerala coast, to be refilled with pepper and other spices in return. So much that these urns (owing to the numbers in which they arrived in Kerala) can be found all over the land even to this day, which are popularly used to preserve salted raw mangoes, locally referred to as *upumanga*.

When the Portuguese began reigning in Kerala, one of their foremost concerns, along with a developed trade, was to propagate the Catholic faith. Christianity was already prevalent in Kerala when the Portuguese arrived at its shores in 1498. St. Thomas Christians (Christians believed to have been converted by the Apostle of Jesus Christ in 1st century AD), who thrived in the ancient sea-port of Muziris, north of Kochi and in today's Thrissur district of Kerala, where religions from faraway lands reached in ships that docked at its harbour, were already following the belief that the Apostle Thomas had instilled in them, and one connected to the Persian church. Nasrani Christians, as they are referred to date, followed stringent food customs that called for specific foods during festivities and fasts. *Pesaha* meal of the Nasranis, a meal during the Holy Week to commemorate the crucifixion of Jesus Christ, called for a special unleavened bread or appam eaten after prayers, shared by the head of the family to its members. The *pesahappam* is made of rice flour and is cooked with a cross—made from palm leaf received on Palm Sunday. The appam is eaten with a dip made of jaggery, cardamom and coconut milk. The ritual of the drinking of bitter herbs, a remembrance of Christ's drink during his journey to the cross, is not part of the *pesaha* ritual but instead is drunk on Good Friday in churches during service. Some of the rituals, it is deemed, were borrowed by the early Christians from the Jewish community in Muziris, of unleavened bread and Passover. (Some scholars on early Christians of Kerala argue that the proclaimed lineage of Syrian Christians to the Brahmans of Kerala is false,

A Syrian Christian wedding photograph from an old family album

since there were no Brahmans in the 1st century in Kerala. Large groups of Syrians never came to Kerala either; it is said that traders married local women, which gave rise to a new community of people that saw a mix of local and Syrian cultures.) Syrian Christian food has a very distinct flavour and history attached to it, known for its spices, meats and breads (appam). The word appam is likely to have originated from the Syriac word *apya;* Syrian Christians of Kerala have a number of breads where the term appam is used, traditional breads that end with the word appam, such as *palappam, neiappam, kaluappam* etc[5].Catholicism, which was brought by travelling missionaries towards the 13th century, was, however, very diluted and weak, and had limited presence in Kerala. When the Portuguese came in the 15th century, they were surprised and distraught by the presence of Christianity they did not approve of. In a rampage to spread Catholicism, they destroyed much of the early evidences of Christianity in Kerala, forced conversions

Vintage photo from an Anglo-Indian family album. Their cuisine was influenced by Portuguese culture, mainly with ingredients and not the cooking style

of Syrian Christians to Catholicism, even offered economic compensation through jobs in the army or the like, to natives who accepted their faith. An outcome of this propaganda was the Synod of Diamper in 1599, to ensure that all homage was paid to the Pope in Rome by all Christians (and not to the patriarch of Babylon). Organised by the Portuguese Bishop Aleixo de Menzes to ensure conversion to Catholicism, he presented a set of laws at Diamper to Syrian priests. The laws were accepted unopposed except for having to say the liturgy in Latin, to which Menzes agreed. However, in 1653, a section of Christians revolted and refused to pay patronage to the Pope in Rome, rebelled and took an oath not to have any religious association with the Portuguese. As a sign of this estrangement, a thick rope was tied to the cross at the Our Lady of Life Church in Mattancherry in Kochi, which was pulled from either side by two separate sections of people—one who vowed not to pay allegiance to Rome, the other who did. The cross bent from the tug, obtained its name *coonan kurishu* meaning 'bent cross', and to this date can be seen at the chapel as a sign of the religious and historic event. The result was the formation of a community of people who embraced distinct characteristics in religious practices. Along with it came lifestyle and food, which were varied, like that of the Latin Catholics, whose food has been enormously influenced by Portuguese cuisine. The Syrians remained different, rejecting Latin rites and following the traditions of their forefathers. Syrian Christian food has a longer history than Latin or Anglo-Indian cuisine, the latter influenced by Portugal culture, was mainly in the form of ingredients introduced to the region and not heavily dependent on Portuguese manner of cooking.

The Latin Catholic community from the author's family album. At an event honouring her grandfather (garlanded). To his right, is the author's grandmother, Annie Burleigh Kurishingal. To his left, is the author's mother, to whom this book is dedicated. Latin Catholics are Keralites in every manner, however, very influenced by the Portuguese settlers

The Latin Catholic community (who settled largely in the coastal areas of ancient trading towns, whilst the Syrians moved to the mainland from seaports like Muziris), have seafood as an important food component. Their cuisine is milder in spice when compared to Syrian Christian food, yet has a local flavour, which makes it uniquely distinguishable. For example, the famed fish dish, *Meen pollichathu* remains heavily different in comparison. Red chillies are absent in the Latin version, spiced only with pepper. Those made in Syrian Christian homes are richer and exude the flavour of a variety of spices, including tamarind for tanginess. As eating of meat was freely accepted among Christians in Kerala (especially beef, though the cow is a sacred animal in India), it became a Sunday must. All meals on Sundays to this day include beef, chicken or pork, where breakfast is lavish with appam or *puttu* (the first made of a fermented rice batter and the second is a steamed cake made of rice-powder), and a local version of the brown stew (introduced later by the British), again of beef or mutton. No red chilli is used in this stew, but is spiced with ginger, pepper, cardamom and cinnamon. Curry leaves and onions add to the flavour, while the meat is cooked in coconut milk.

One can also distinguish between Anglo-Indian food and those found in Latin homes; however they are also similar, sharing common flavours and even dishes. Traditions of Latin lineage and its influence on cooking can be seen to date, of spice usage and rituals that have a similarity to Portuguese traditions. Specifically found in such communities is the *kodalu* curry, made of cow intestines and liver, commonly during religious feasts, like Vanakamasam—the feast of Mother Mary in the month of May and not necessarily Christmas or Easter, which calls for more flamboyant preparations. There is little doubt that the Portuguese have left a strong impact on the cuisine of Kerala. And as the first colonisers, they have left an indelible mark upon Kerala society.

The Portuguese are given credit for the invention of *puttu*, a steamed rice cake, today one of the most popular Kerala staples. Made of rice powder, the story goes that when the Portuguese needed to feed the numerous men of its army, rice was powdered and steamed in cylindrical bamboo pipes, which was easily cooked over a pot of boiling water on ships. The addition of coconut to *puttu* makes it a Kerala specialty; today *puttu* is eaten with an array of curries across Kerala, mainly as a breakfast staple.

Dutch Power, Arrival of the English, Rise of Anglo-Indians

When the Dutch invaded Cochin in 1653, they were determined to wipe out all Portuguese influence. Many buildings, including friaries, libraries and houses were brought down. Street names were changed from Portuguese to Dutch. However, two prominent aspects that could not be erased completely were Catholicism and the other, food. If we trace history, we see that even today, amongst the various foreign influenced cuisines, it is Portuguese cuisine that has survived the test of time. For one, Dutch reign was tight and contained. They had not opted for an open marriage-policy like what the Portuguese authorities had initiated. Portuguese customs had seeped deep into society, and by the time the Dutch arrived, a strong Indo-Portuguese community had developed with traditions and a culture of their own. So, even when Portuguese rule ended in Kerala, there existed in places like Cochin descendants who kept their influence alive.

The Dutch lived a life of flamboyance and great leisure. They built summerhouses, and food and drink was an essential part of their lifestyle. An account by M. Anguetil du Perron, a French author who stayed in Fort Cochin toward the end of 1757 describes their lifestyle of extravagance, where dinners included glasses of undiluted brandy, beer, and wine, followed by tobacco pipes. Describing the tavern-keeper in Fort Cochin who entertained guests a great deal, he says, 'Dining seemed to be the great event in his life, attended by two kaffirs, and four little Negroes, of which one poured out his potations, another wiped his mouth, and the third chased away the flies, whilst the fourth fanned him.' However, little speak of Dutch influenced

Consumption of bread and cakes like the brudher *in Fort Cochin is an old tradition. The name hails from the Dutch bread* brodjee

local food in Kerala. Of the few, Brudher (Brudher is a sweet cake with dried plums and comes from the word *brodjee*, meaning bread in Dutch) and the potato cutlet (close to the Dutch *kroketten* or croquettes) are what are popularly consumed in places like Fort Cochin. A host of Dutch biscuits were made, of which *kokis*, a hard cake of rice flour and coconut milk–from the Dutch word *coekje*–or cookies was popular (it is believed from here originated *achappam* or rose cookies, a very popular sweet snack of Kerala), and traditional alcohol existed as part of the cuisine but consequently died a slow death once the Dutch departed from Kerala. But certain Malayalam words like *panni* are still in use in Kerala–pertaining to the 'Dutch pig'–which was once popularly cooked in Kerala[6].

The Dutch were followed by the English, who set up establishments and spread their political interests throughout the country, by early 19th century. Most of the English who came to British-India were men, interested in making money or in pursuit of political and administrative ideas. It was rare to find English women in India during the late 18th and 19th centuries and marriages with local women became a common practice. The children from such English alliances were specifically called Eurasians (later having fallen under a common term—'Anglo-Indians in Kerala' **III**), who, however, towards the middle of the 19th century, lost importance in society, once English women could easily reach Indian shores. Alliances with natives were heavily discouraged and both the British government and the Indians ignored the well-being of this mixed race. In Kerala, the arrival of the English was at a time when open alliances with native women were on a decline; it was not all that common, like it was with the Portuguese, to find Anglo-Indians of British descent. Women from Great Britain were shipped to India to marry eligible bachelors. Others, who had been pining for their husbands in England, quickly arrived to a country of new cultures and traditions. It is said that the heat, humidity, dirt and dust were staunch enemies to an English woman's delicate skin and heavy clothing. Yet, many fitted in, and with an entourage of servants, built a life flavoured with India and England.

Food was an important aspect of the lives of these women, elaborately developed to display the status and power of many a hostess. When they initially arrived in India, the spicy masala and pungent curries were rejected in distaste. The introduction of English food was quick, with desperate efforts to train cooks to serve recipes from Britain with little or no familiar ingredients available. The result of this attempt was, however, far from the original. It was difficult to pluck the brown skinned spice lover out of his love for the curry. Nor was it easy to create English flavours with Indian produce. (Ingredients for English food, if any, were never fresh, and were

Streetscape of the Malabar region of Kerala, in Kannur. The busy and narrow street is a blend of local traditional attire and architecture

parcelled from larger cities like Bombay [Mumbai] to Kerala.) Popular even to this day are the spiced shepherd's pie and cardamom flavoured caramel pudding. Pork chops were marinated with spices and then grilled, and new flavours of soups were made with local spices. Pepper water, for example, is made of beef stock, with freshly crushed black pepper and shallots. There were also a number of beverages that became popular in Kerala over time. The British introduced whisky and only the very wealthy Indians could afford Scotch. One story goes that since ice was specially shipped from Britain to enjoy a glass of whisky, the cost of procuring ice was as much as the whisky itself[7]! But amongst beverages, the universal and most popular prevailing influence of the English was the afternoon tea. Tea, although known to have been brought to India by the Chinese centuries earlier, came to influence the lifestyle of Indians in a wide scale only after the British introduced the popular English custom of tea drinking in this country. In Kerala, it is a milky, sweet version that is widely enjoyed, available at both roadside tea stalls as well as prominent restaurants, which host elaborate tea-drinking practices.

Cooks, thus, adorned important roles in homes, with kitchens often placed outside the main house under thatched roofs amidst firewood and thick smoke. The ladies of these houses, until satisfied that the cook was capable of taking care of things himself, regularly supervised them. Cooks or *kokies*, as they were known locally, were responsible for conjuring up a menu every day, which required them to use their creativity to present favourable and new dishes, which very often, was an English dish with a sprinkle of Indian taste or vice versa. The 'dish' became a fancied topic of conversation, raised to the position of an elite prodigy of the local curry, the genius of one cook compared to that of another, at dinner parties. To serve a dish, eventually, became fashionable in native homes. Many natives imitated the Westerners and years after the English left India, the *kokie*, with his special knowledge of a unique cuisine, continued to hold important positions in kitchens across Kerala.

Jews of Kerala

Late Sarah Cohen at her home in Jew Town. She was one of the last of the Paradesi Jews of Kochi till her death in August 2019

The first Jews arrived in India, in Muziris, from the Middle East (**I**). These 'Dark Jews' or 'Malabari Jews' as they are called to date, were granted the rights to flourish as a community by the local rajah, offering permission to trade, build synagogues and build houses. The 'White Jews' arrived much later; Historian MGS Narayanan says they came from Spain and Portugal in the 15th and 16th centuries[8].The Jews thrived here for many years, making Muziris and the surrounding regions their home. However, in the 16th century, because of Portuguese tyranny, many of them fled to Cochin (obtaining protection from its rajah) and other surrounding regions. In Jew Town, in Mattancherry, they cultivated their faith and culture on a few streets; the Paradesi Synagogue ('Paradesi' meaning foreigner, referring to the 'White Jews') and the Clock Tower were both built in the 16th century next to the Cochin rajah's temple and palace. However, today, only vestiges remain of the Malabari synagogues in Mattancherry; the neighbouring city of Ernakulum continues to house them, including the 800 year-old Kadavumbagam Synagogue. Few remain of both sections of people in Kerala today, most of them having left after the formation of the State of Israel in 1948 (**II**). Yet, the presence they carry of Kerala is strongly visible in Israel, where the community continues to practice traditions of their forefathers, including cooking food of Kerala flavour. As customs were preserved, both amongst the Jews in Kerala and Israel, there was a deep sense of commitment and dedication to their ancestry and food continues to be used to celebrate or mark a significant event.

Kerala based dishes still find place on tables in Israel, prepared from cookbooks handed down generations, and relished over a conversation

Old photograph of Malabari Jews welcoming a delegate at their synagogue. From the album of a family that left Kerala for Israel

in Malayalam (Early Jews spoke Shingly, a Judai-Malayalam language. In later years, this gave way to the easiness of adopting Malayalam as a means of conversation. Children were taught both Hebrew and Malayalam in equal earnest, teachers appointed solely for the purpose). When it came to religion, the Jews in Kerala adhered to Kosher laws with utmost obedience. For Passover, forbidden grains like wheat, oats, rye, barley and spelt were removed a month earlier from homes and the utensils used for cooking were replaced with new ones. Dairy was forbidden completely and in its place Kerala Jewish women used coconut milk that proved to be a fine substitute. The use of such ingredients changed traditional Jewish recipes significantly. *Kubba* meaning 'ball' in Arabic, originated in Baghdad and Cochinni Jews made it with ground meat (beef or fish) to which were added onions and spices and then encased in rice flour dough and cooked in a gravy consisting of gourd and okra. 'Interestingly, pastel, a very popular Jewish snack, is made to this day in Cochinni Jewish homes,' mentions Shlomo Reinman in the book *Masa'oth Shlomo b'Kogin*[9].

A Syrian Catholic wedding photograph from Dr Eapen Thomas's album. Syrian Christians converted the Jewish bread to the popular appam in Kerala

Cochin Jews have been cooking dishes like *ispethi* (red beef stew), for centuries. Some dishes are similar to those of Christians and Muslims due to the close proximity of the communities in ancient trade ports, but stand out significantly solely because of their Jewish heritage. As in other Kerala communities, bread was a

The Jew Town in Kochi is still a vibrant space with tourists from all over the world coming here for the ethnic food and artefacts

popular item amongst Jews. Instead of yeast, coconut toddy was used to ferment the dough and baked in what was called *pornas*, which came from the Spanish word *horno*[10]. It is said that Kerala's quintessential bread, appam, originated in Jewish homes in ancient Kerala and were later made popular by Syrian Christians. Interestingly, the mention of food has been noted in the Jewish women's folksongs sung in Malayalam, mainly in reference to bread (based on stories in the Torah). Linguist scholar and an expert in the study of these folksongs, Dr Scaria Zacharia says that at the time of a woman's marriage she was given a customary book by her mother, which contained the lyrics to these songs and recipes of the family that were handed down generations. Forty-eight of these books, he says, can be found in the archives of the Hebrew University in Israel, those that left the shores of Kerala for safekeeping and research.

A number of food items were the same or similar to those prepared by other Kerala communities. Like *achappam*, *unniappam*, and *neiappam*,

Shared from the archives of Mathrubhumi, a Kerala publishing house, this photograph shows Mappila men with visitors from the West

which the Jews prepared during Hannukah, a popular treat during the festival. Jewish version of the Muslim sweet *muttamala*, called *motta salada*, was made during weddings. The Jews also made halwa (said to have come from the Middle East) commonly seen in the Muslim communities in Kerala .One version of the halwa, is the Jewish *alw*, a sweet made of semolina, containing no milk (it is *parve*, and thus the avoidance of dairy) and shared amongst the members of the community during Rosh Hashanah. During the Day of Atonement, the Jews fasted for 27 days, which was eventually broken with a preparation similar to the halwa, a pudding made of wheat and called *ural*. When a family member dies, a hot drink called *mooli*, made from spices like coriander seeds, cumin, cinnamon and cardamom mixed with sugar is consumed[11]. *Duwoo* is a specific *charoset*[12], a symbolic food of Passover, made during Passover with locally available dates and is sweeter than the original version and contains wine and cinnamon.

Mappila male musicians performing. Whilst women took care of the household, public exposure for a long time, was reserved for the menfolk

Arrival of Arab Traders in Kerala

Islam came to Kerala with the arrival of Muslim traders from the Middle East to its shores in search of spices. These Arab merchants controlled spice trade for a long time in Kerala, till the formation of the Roman Empire and the onset of European seafarers to the East in search of new trade prospects[13]. Their influence in Kerala is one of the oldest, and played a key role in the ancient trade developments in the region. Goods traded with Kerala are recorded in the Old Testament (during the period of Solomon), noted as Ophir (today known as Beypore in Malabar)[14].

It was the geographical advantage of the region that lured traders, who, through the straits of Malacca, sailed to China and then to Kerala. Calicut was a perfect destination for the storage of trade-goods and a place of rest for traders, a transit point that witnessed Arab traders settling in the region for periods of time, owing to special permissions for trade granted by the Zamorin of Calicut. A new community emerged from alliances

Matriarchs of the Mappila women at a social event. They ran the household, taking full charge and the cuisine found chance for new innovations

of local women with Arab men and their children were often referred to as Mappila. The word Mappila has two versions associated with its origin. One refers to the bridegroom, the other meaning is derived from 'Ma-pillai' or 'children of mothers', whose paternal lineage was a blur since Arab traders never stayed for long periods of time in the Malabar. The Mappila community is one of Kerala's dominant groups of people today, with specific cultures and traditions that find their links to Islam. The community connects its cuisine's flavour to the Middle East in the use of ingredients, method of cooking and traditions of eating. Traditionally, Mappila communities followed the matriarchal system, property was co-owned by the women of a family and lineage was through the mother alone. Women adorned roles that were powerful and significant in a household. With homes housing very large families, often up to 150-200 members at a time, kitchens played a significant role in the everyday lives of the Mappila people. Women once married continued living in their homes with their husbands and children. This gave them the freedom and power to hire kitchen help and experiment with food freely. Following the Quran's instruction regarding food, the Malabar Muslims believed in communal eating. This is especially seen during weddings, when a *supra*, which is a circular palm leaf mat, is placed on the ground and a gathering of eight to 10 men sit around a large plate and eat together. Wedding food is extensive, with an array of snacks fried, grilled and steamed. Plates of traditional breads like *pathiri*, appam and paratha are eaten with meat dishes, followed by the popular Malabar mutton biryani served with chutneys, a curd based salad and date pickle. This biryani stands out from the Mughal version. The latter used curd and spices to marinate the meat, while the Malabar uses eight special spices to cook the meat (mutton, chicken or seafood). After a wedding, the bridegroom is referred to as *puthiyappila* or 'new boy', a name he carries for the remaining of his life. Breakfast the day after the wedding is a celebrated meal, where the *puthiyappila* is fed with boiled eggs and sautéed bananas; customary eats at his first breakfast in the bride's home. This is followed with *pathiri* and snacks like liver fry, brain masala, and chicken curry to name a few, followed by various sweetmeats. This celebration continues for the 40 days where the arrival of the 'new boy' is celebrated in great festivity.

Drawing from the presence of Arab traders since the 8th century in Malabar who used to station in Kerala, setting up trade centres and families with local women, local food transformed into a unique cuisine distinct to the region alone. The tradition of stuffing meats is seen in dishes prepared for festive occasions (which include a whole chicken stuffed with eggs, grilled and encased in dough, similar to the stuffing of a camel with a goat and then chicken in Arabia). Biryani is another specialty, a recipe unseen in the rest of India. Adopting Arab traditions and blending it with locally available ingredients, biryani from the Malabar possesses a unique taste that has been passed down generations. The use of dates and grilling food is a tradition not common in Kerala but the Muslim community follows it to date. Breads are common in a meal, following the tradition of eating them in Arabia, but made mostly of rice, a local Kerala produce. The tradition of layering in Arabic sweets is also found in the Malabar region in its famed sweet *chatti pathiri*. Sulaimani tea is a special tea, where black tea is flavoured with lime, sugar, cinnamon and saffron, brewing it till the right shade of gold is obtained. While the rest of Kerala leaned towards the use of coconut oil in their cooking, Mappila food uses ghee in many of their recipes, absorbed from Arab practices. Moreover, meat porridge known as *alisa* and the grinding of wheat to make dishes are obvious influences from Arabia. It is said that the tradition of using ghee in a land where coconut oil was mostly consumed may have come from Arabia (where a nomadic Arabian group called Samn use ghee in their cooking). Historian and expert on the Malabar, Dr KKN Kurup, however, debates that the use of ghee in food is originally a tradition of Kerala, used by the men of the Mappila community who went out to sea for long periods of time (the men in the community were famed for their skills as seafarers and fighters par excellence in the Zamorin's army [**IV**], christened as his special navy). Kurup holds that an easy, energy providing and nutritious food was prepared with the addition of ghee to well-cooked rice that was consumed on ships in copious quantities. This, he holds, is the base for development of dishes like *alisa*, commonly eaten in Muslim Malabar communities to date. Being seafarers, fish is an important part of their cuisine[15]. Fish is consumed as a simple curry on a daily basis, where it is fermented using tamarind, raw-mango or tomato, just like in the rest of Kerala. However, the use of gooseberry in fish is something quite unique to their cuisine.

The Malabar Muslim community is a unique Muslim community in India. They have their own version of Malayalam known as Arabi Malayalam, the letters of which are in Arabic, an alphabet that was used in the absence of Malayalam letters[16]. Food is an important part of the community's life, where fasting and feasting are both followed with great attention. Every kitchen is robust with activity, preparing snacks for each evening during the month of Ramzan, when a daylong fast is broken. Snacks are numerous in number, ensuring the household is well fed to withstand the next day's fasting. A variety of the same food-item is found in the cuisine of the Malabar Muslims. For example, there are 50 different types of *pathiri* (bread made of rice flour, rolled to a fine texture and grilled) alone. Some differentiate in the fillings used, like in the case of samosa, others maybe fried or steamed snacks, each of which carries a different flavour. The Malabar community of Arab descendants is famed for their skill of merging spices and other ingredients, both sourced locally and brought on ships to Kerala shores. Like the Jews, Christians and the Anglo-Indians, they too are extremely proud of their ancestry and cherish the traditions associated with it.

Whilst communities like the Jews are on the verge of disappearance from Kerala after so many centuries, others continue to flourish with unique identities. Kerala may bid goodbye to the last generation of its Jews in the next couple of years. But it can continue to regale in their presence through the living heritage of food. To think that spices lured new religions and customs, to create new sections of peoples in the tiny state of Kerala in peninsular India, the one common ingredient that established their presence strongly, which influenced the evolution of cuisines and bear distinctive characteristics, is a story that calls for safekeeping. Both for history and in memory of those who brought to life new tastes that continue to hold together a past of great global significance.

Endnotes

I. One version regarding the arrival of the Jews says they came on the ships of King Solomon that docked on the Muziris coast for trade around 3000 years ago. Another speaks about the arrival of the Jews in the 6th century, after the destruction of the First Temple; some records, mainly oral history, say that they fled to Malabar after the destruction of the Second Temple in the 1st century. Others say they came in the 4th and 5th centuries from Majorca in Spain, but the first written evidence of the Jews in Kerala is only in the 9th and 11th centuries, noted in the inscriptions on the copper plates which stated certain privileges given to the community by the ruling king. One recording (evidence from a Jewish Malayalam folk song sung by women) suggests the coming of a community from Yemen who travelled upland to Calicut. The last arrival of the Jews is said to date back to the 16th century AD in Kodungallur, a migration of Sephardi or Sephardic Jews, which took place from Spain and Portugal. This community of Jews set up their own community of traditions and did not associate freely with the prevailing Jewish community. The first documented evidence of the Sephardi Jews dates back to 1000 CE, an agreement given to Joseph Rabban of the Paradesi community by the local rajah. As a result of this alliance, there were eventually eight synagogues in Kerala, where resided communities of Jews with specific traditions and rituals

II. The two communities of Jews in Kerala, the Paradesi and Malabari, never mingled and led separate lives. Looked down upon by the fairer skinned community, the Malabari Jews were often treated in disdain and not allowed to worship in the Paradesi synagogue for a very long time. Malabari Jews, however, preserve and cherish their authority in the land as the first to have reached Kerala shores, as far back as the 5th century. Ref:https://www.ncbi.nlm.nih.gov/pmc/articles/PMC5020127/

III. Article 366 [2] of the Indian Constitution explains an Anglo-Indian to be one of European decent which includes of British decent, so also of Portuguese, Dutch and French decent.

IV. Zamorin or Samoodries of Calicut were the rulers of the Malabar, very powerful kings of the time who encouraged open trade policies.

References:

1 Abraham, Tanya, Fort Cochin, *History and Untold Stories*, Ink on Paper, 2010.

(I) (II) 2 Malekandathil, Pius, *Cultural and Political Meanings of Pepper during Pre-Modern Period*, Indian Horizons, Vol 63,No 3,July-September 2016.

(III) 3 Menon, Sreedhara, *A Survey of Kerala History*, D C Books, 2008.

4 Abraham, Tanya, Fort Cochin, *History and Untold Stories*, Ink on Paper, 2010.

5 https://www.nasrani.net/2012/11/11/pesaha-celebration-of-nasranis-a-socio-cultural-analysis/.

6 Koder, S.S, 'Glimpses of Cochin', *Fort Cochin Municipal Centenary Souvenir*. Fort Cochin. Cochin, 1966.

7 Abraham, Tanya, Fort Cochin, *History and Untold Stories*, Ink on Paper, 2010.

8 M.G.S., Narayanan, *Cultural Symbiosis in Kerala* (Trivandrum: Kerala Historical Society, 1972).

9 https://cafedissensus.com/?s=Masa'oth+Shlomo+b'Kogin.

10 Menon, Bala, *Spice & Kosher, Exotic Cuisine of the Cochin Jews*, 2013.

11 https://cafedissensus.com/2014/12/31/the-cochini-jewish-cuisine/.

12 Daniel, Ruby & Barbara Johnson, *Ruby of Cochin: An Indian Jewish Woman Remembers*, Jewish Publication Society of America, 2002.

13 Kunju, A.P. Ebrahim, *Studies in Medieval Kerala History* (Thiruvananthapuram: 1975).

14 Bahaudhin, K.M., *Kerala Muslingal: Poraattathinte Charitram*, Islamic Publishing House, 1995.

15 Kurup K.K.N., personal interview to author, Kochi, 20 September, 2017.

16 Kurup K.K.N., personal interview to author, Kochi, 20 September, 2017.

Quaint, old world Kochi houses give way to new ventures in the business of food and art

way to the table~the recipes

VEGETABLES

pal peechinga curry

RIDGE GOURD IN COCONUT MILK

Latin Catholic; Annie Burleigh Kurishingal

A light and fresh curry, the flavour of coconut milk is highlighted with the subtle use of spices

Ridge gourd ~ 1, medium size
Garlic ~ 3-4, flakes
Onion ~ 1, sliced
Mustard seeds ~ A pinch
Green chillies ~ 3, slit
Coconut milk ~ 1 coconut, first and second milk
Oil ~ 3 tbsp
Salt ~ to taste

Clean the gourd and slice. Heat oil in a shallow vessel and splutter the mustard seeds. Add the onions, garlic, and green chillies. When cooked, add the gourd slices, salt and the second milk. Reduce heat and allow it to cook. When done, add the first milk and boil on low flame till a semi-thick gravy is obtained.

peechinga chamandi

RIDGE GOURD CHUTNEY

Anglo-Indian, Mertel Gomez

A tangy preparation, this is a quick and easy dish prepared on the arrival of last-minute guests. Another version is the addition of coconut milk to it and the omission of tamarind

Ridge gourd ~ 1
Green chillies ~ 1-2,
as per taste for hot, spicy flavour
Shallots ~ 8, four for seasoning
Ginger ~ ½ inch
Tamarind ~ small piece,
soaked in a little water
Salt ~ as required

Skin the gourd. And to this, add the chilli powder, green chillies, shallots, garlic and ginger. Grind these using tamarind water and salt. Season with remaining shallots using oil.

mousad

MUSTARD SAUCE

Anglo-Indian, Mertel Gomez

This is a great accompaniment to meats and a must in Anglo-Indian homes

Cleaned mustard seeds ~ 2 tbsp
Dried chilli seeds ~ 1 tbsp
Garlic cloves ~ 10
Drumstick bark ~ 1 piece (1½ square size)
Ginger ~ 4 slices
Vinegar, salt and sugar ~ to taste
Peppercorns ~ 4
Cloves ~ 3
Cinnamon ~ a small piece

Powder the drumstick bark, cloves, peppercorns, cinnamon. Grind it along with the remaining ingredients till a thick sauce is formed.

vazhaka mezhakuperatiyathu

GREEN BANANA CURRY

Syrian Christian, Sarala Thomas Pallivathukal

This dish can be served dry, allowing all the water to evaporate or as a very thick curry by allowing some of the water to remain

Unripe green bananas ~ 3, large
Water ~ 2½ cups to cook and 1 cup to soak the bananas
Turmeric powder ~ ½ tsp
Garlic ~ 4 cloves
Crushed red chilli powder ~ ¾ tsp
Shallots ~ 5, diced
Mustard seeds ~ ¼ tsp
Curry leaves ~ a few
Oil ~ 2 tbsp
Salt ~ to taste

Dice the bananas with the outer-skin and put them in a bowl of water till use (to avoid discolourisation). In a vessel, cook the banana pieces with turmeric, crushed red chillies and salt, and cook till done. Splutter the mustard seeds in oil. Add the garlic, shallots and curry leaves and sauté. Add the cooked banana pieces and continue cooking, making sure the banana does not stick to the vessel.

vendakai thengapal

OKRA IN COCONUT MILK

Syrian Christian, Mary Mathew Madathikunnel

A thick curry used as an accompaniment to rice, the addition of coriander adds a unique flavour

Ladies finger ~ ¼ kg, sliced into 1″ sizes
Onion ~ 1, sliced
Green chillies ~ 3, slit
Garlic ~ 3, sliced
Ginger ~ ½, sliced fine
Coriander powder ~ 2 tsp, heaped
Chilli powder ~ ¼ tsp
Turmeric powder ~ ⅛ tsp
Garam masala ~ ½ tsp
Coconut milk ~ 1 coconut, first and second milk
Oil ~ 2 tsp
Salt ~ to taste
Vinegar ~ ¼ tsp or to taste

Sauté ladies finger in a little oil and remove from the pan.

Sauté the sliced onions, green chillies, curry leaves, garlic and ginger till the onion changes colour. Add all the powders and sauté.

Now, add the second coconut milk, the fried ladies finger and salt. When cooked over medium flame, add a little vinegar and the first milk. Remove from fire just before it begins to boil.

uppu manga chaaru

SALTED GREEN MANGO CURRY

Syrian Christian, Parayil family

Uppu manga is found in every Kerala Christian home. During mango season, green mangoes are preserved in potent salt water in large ceramic urns. Over time the mangoes turn salty and this preserve, used for cooking lasts a year or more

Uppu manga ~ 2 (salted green mango)
Shallots ~ 8
Green chillies ~ 3, diced
Ginger ~ 1 small piece, sliced fine
Milk of one coconut

To salt the mangoes

Unripe, green mangoes
Rock salt
Water
Salt and water ~ in proportion

Boil the water and when lukewarm, add the salt to it, stirring to dissolve. When cool, pour the water into an urn or large glass bottle. Add the mangoes and close the lid.

Let it remain for at least a month or more before using.

To prepare the curry

Slice the salted mango and add all the ingredients to it. Mix all ingredients well and serve.

lime raisin pickle

Syrian Christian, Mary Mathew Madathikunnel

Lime skin from used lime is preserved in salted water and used to make pickle once the jar is full. Lime pickle is synonymous with every Kerala home. Another version avoids red chilli powder and uses dry red chillies only. The raisins add the mild sweetness to the pickle

Lime ~ 12
Sugar ~ 2 tsp
Gingelly (or sesame) oil ~ ¼ cup
Mustard seed ~ ½ tsp
Fenugreek seeds ~ ½ tsp
Dry red chillies ~ 3 (cut into two pieces)
Ginger ~ 1½ inch long, sliced
Garlic ~ 1 pod, sliced
Raisins ~ ½ cup
Kashmiri chilli powder ~ 2 tbsp
Fenugreek powder ~ ½ tsp
Asafoetida powder ~ ½ tsp
Sugar ~ 2 tsp
Hot water ~ ½ cup
Vinegar
Salt ~ to taste

Cut the lime into 8 pieces.

Keep them in a jar with salt and sugar for 3-4 hours.

Heat the gingelly oil and add to it the mustard seeds and red chillies. Next add the ginger and garlic and sauté till light brown.

Reduce the heat and add chilli powder, fenugreek and asafoetida along with the sugar. Add the raisins and mix well. Finally add the vinegar, salt and hot water.

Add the lime and stir well.

Take the pan off the fire and when it cools transfer into a glass or ceramic jar.

salas

ONIONS SALAD

Syrian Christian, Mary Mathew Madathikunnel

Salas is also referred to as the common man's salad. Salads are not part of Kerala cuisine owing to the variety of vegetarian preparations. This recipe is not meant to be too sour, thus the vinegar must be added according to one's need. A few grains of sugar bring out the flavour well. Can be made without the coconut milk as well

Big onion ~ 1, sliced very thin
Green chillies ~ 1, cut round finely
Vinegar ~ to taste
Salt ~ to taste
Coconut milk ~ ¼ cup, first milk

Rub the onion slices with salt till it becomes a little soft. Add green chillies, a little vinegar, and thick coconut milk. Mix well and serve with the main dishes.

BREADS, RICE AND APPAMS WITH CHUTNEYS

aripodi roti

UNLEAVENED BREAD

Syrian Christian,
Mary Mathew Madathikunnel

This roti is eaten with curry or with a mixture of ghee and sugar during teatime

Rice flour ~ 2 cups
Water ~ 1½ cups
Coconut ~ ½ cup, grated
Salt ~ to taste

Boil the water with salt. Pour the water into the rice flour along with the coconut scrapings and sugar. Mix it and form crumbles. The texture should be crumbly. Knead the mixture well to make a thick dough. Flatten the dough to one inch thickness and gently transfer to a pan lined with an oiled banana leaf. Cover with another leaf and let the roti cook over medium flame till a crust is formed.

kaiveesal

EGG JALEBI APPAM

Malabar Mappila, Rasheeda and Rahima Meethalakath

In days of yore, a coconut shell was used instead of a paper cone, in which a hole was made at the bottom to make kaiveesal. It is often eaten as an iftar snack

All purpose flour (maida) ~ 1 cup
Eggs ~ 4
Sugar ~ 4 tbsp
Oil ~ for deep-frying
Salt ~ a pinch

Beat the eggs and sugar well. Add the flour and mix well.

Heat the oil and pour the batter through an icing cone in a circular manner to make small to medium sized rounds. Strain the oil well from the discs and remove them from fire when their colour turns a rich golden brown.

orotti rice bread

UNLEAVENED BREAD

Malabar Mappila, Rasheeda and Rahima Meethalakath

The original recipe calls for two types of rice–ponni and pacha– to be boiled and ground to a thick paste. The availability of roasted rice powder has made making orotti a much easier task. Orotti is eaten with curries, ishtew, and even with milk and sugar

Rice flour ~ 2 cups
Water ~ 1½ cups
Coconut ~ ½ cup, grated
Salt ~ to taste

Boil the water and add the salt and grated coconut to it. Take it off the fire and gradually add the rice flour stirring to make a thick dough.

Knead the dough to a smooth consistency. Make small to medium sized balls with your palms, dipping them in water if the balls need to be moist.

Roll into thin flat discs and cook on a hot griddle. Use oil to grease if needed.

kappa vevichathu

TAPIOCA IN COCONUT

Syrian Christian, Mary Mathew Madathikunnel

This recipe can also be made without the coconut milk, which would be of a drier consistency than with it. It is popularly served with red fish curry. Details on kappa (tapioca) given in the next recipe (p.66)

Kappa ~ 1 kg
Coconut ~ ½ cup, grated
Coconut milk ~ 1 cup, first milk
Garlic ~ 1-2 cloves
Cumin seeds ~ 10
Curry leaves ~ a few
Small onions ~ 10
Oil ~ To splutter spices
Water and salt ~ to cook tapioca
Salt ~ to taste

Boil the tapioca in enough water and add a teaspoon of salt. Once cooked, let it cool. Remove the skin, mash with the back of a ladle or with fingers.

Add the grated coconut and milk to the cooked tapioca. Heat the oil and splutter the cumin.

Add the garlic and the shallots. Last, add the curry leaves. Pour the oil with all the spices into the tapioca and mix well.

kappa chamandi

TAPIOCA WITH CHUTNEY

Syrian Christian, Mary Mathew Madathikunnel

Tapioca came from South America through Portuguese trade, to Kerala.The vessel for boiling tapioca is called urali. Kappa is a favourite of Kerala's Syrian Christians. Eaten for lunch with fish or meat or as a teatime snack, kappa can replace rice as a staple. A semi-dry beef curry can be mixed with kappa puzhuku

Kappa/Tapioca ~ 1 kg, 2" pieces
Water and salt ~ to cook the tapioca
Cook the tapioca, peel and keep aside.

for the chutney

Uli chamandi/Spicy chutney with shallots
Shallots ~ 1 cup
Vinegar ~ 1 tbsp
Green chillies ~ 2 (increase the number for more spice)
Coconut oil ~ 1½ teaspoon
Salt ~ to taste (a sprinkle only)

Grind the shallots and chillies together to form a paste. Add coconut oil, vinegar and salt and mix well. Serve with the kappa.

unaka mulagu chamandi

DRY RED CHILLI CHUTNEY

Syrian Christian, Mary Mathew Madathikunnel

A pungent chutney, it is an ideal accompaniment to tapioca (kappa), even rice gruel (kanji)

Red chillies ~ 7
Shallots ~ 7-8, peeled and whole
Tamarind ~ size of a small ball, equal to a teaspoonful
Coconut oil ~ 1 tsp
Turmeric powder ~ a pinch (optional)
Vinegar ~ 1 tablespoon
Curry leaves ~ 6
Salt ~ to taste

Heat the oil and roast the chillies till they slightly turn colour. Add the shallots and curry leaves and once cooked, remove from fire. Add the tamarind to it when cool and grind to a fine paste (a little water can be added if the paste is too dry). Add the vinegar, salt and the turmeric powder and mix well.

coconut rice

Anglo-Indian, Howard La'frenais

This preparation is eaten on its own or with a curry. The flavour of the coconut milk and spices makes the preparation unique

Rice ~ 2 cups
Coconut milk ~ 3 cups
Cardamom ~ 5
Cinnamon ~ 2 pieces
Cloves ~ 5
Saffron ~ 1 tsp
Ghee ~ 4 tbsp
Salt ~ to taste

In a pot, add all of the above ingredients. Cook till done. If rice is being made in a pressure cooker, let the ingredients come to a boil. Place the lid of the pressure cooker with the weight. Allow it to whistle for 4 minutes on high flame and the next 4 minutes on low flame. Turn off the heat after the last minute, and allow it to cool for the rice to be perfectly cooked.

pinjanathappam

EGG WHITE PUDDING OR BREAD

Malabar Mappila, Rasheeda and Rahima Meethalakath

This is an accompaniment to muttamala which resembles yellow noodles and are intricate loops made of egg yolk. This combination makes it the ultimate dessert. Some recipes include milk and ghee. Some households also eat it as bread with curry

Egg ~ 12, whites only (the yolks are used for the muttamala)
Cardamom ~ ½ tsp (or as required)
Remaining sugar syrup of muttamala

Separate the egg whites from the yolks and beat well. Once fluffy, add the sugar syrup and the cardamom powder and continue beating. This is the bread or pudding mixture. Steam the mixture in a pan and once cooked and cooled, cut the bread into diamond shapes.

Serve as pudding with muttamala or as bread with curry.

indri or pesaha appam

UNLEAVENED BREAD

Syrian Christian, Sarala Thomas Palivathukkal

Pesaha vyazhacha refers to Maundy Thursday. Prepared on Maundy Thursday, this unleavened bread is made with great solemnity, by the women of the household. The bread is cooked by placing a cross made from the palm leaf received on Palm Sunday. In the evening, the male head of the family breaks the bread after prayers and shares it with his family to commemorate the Last Supper. The bread is eaten with a jaggery sauce

Rice flour ~ 1 cup
Coconut ~ 1 cup, grated
Urunu parripu (urad dal) ~ ¼ cup, soaked for 20 minutes
Shallots ~ 3
Garlic cloves ~ 4
Cumin ~ A pinch
Water ~ 1½ cups
Salt ~ to taste

jaggery sauce

Rice powder ~ ½ cup
Coconut milk ~ 1 cup, first milk (thick milk)
Coconut milk ~ 2 cups, second milk
Jaggery ~ 350 gm
Cardamom ~ 2
Cumin seeds (whole) ~ ½ tsp
Water ~ as required

Mix the rice flour with salt. Grind the urunu parripu (urad dal) with a little water to form a paste. Add the paste to the flour. Grind the coconut with the cumin and add to the rice mixture. Add the garlic, shallots and water to make a semi-thick batter. Pour the batter in a shallow mould and steam.

for the jaggery sauce

Break the jaggery into pieces and melt in low heat with water. Once it melts, strain and keep the liquid aside. Mix the rice flour in the second milk and add to the jaggery. Heat over low flame till the liquid thickens, stirring constantly. Add the cumin and cardamom to it and let it simmer for about a minute. Switch the flame off and pour the first coconut milk. Serve warm or at room temperature.

On Bazaar Road in Mattancherry which houses remnants of the spice market, a woman cleans pepper before storing it

naranga choru

RICE WITH LIME AND SPICES

Malabari Jews, Ilanit Menachem

This is a tangy rice, flavoured with spices. Unique to the Jews, this recipe is used mainly during festivals and events of celebration

Basmati rice ~ 2 cups
Oil ~ 2 tbsp
Lime juice ~ 1 large lime
Black mustard seeds ~ 1 tsp
Chickpea lentils ~ 1 tbsp
Peanuts or cashew nuts ~ ½ cup
Peppercorns ~ a few
Green chillies ~ 1, chopped
Cumin seeds ~ a large pinch
Coriander seeds ~ 1 tsp
Garlic ~ 2 cloves
Ginger ~ 1 tsp
Salt ~ 1 tsp
Coriander leaves for garnish

Cook the rice with the turmeric and salt and keep aside. Heat oil in a frying pan and fry the lentils, nuts, cumin, coriander and pepper on low flame. Add the remaining ingredients and cook well ensuring not to burn the ginger. Remove from the heat and cool. Pour the mixture over the rice and sprinkle the limejuice. Mix well. Garnish with coriander leaves (optional).

plav

COCONUT AND CHICKEN RICE

Paradesi Jews, Queenie Hallegua

Plav is made on special occasions, a simple yet rich staple which can be eaten even on its own

Raw rice ~ 1 cup
Coconut milk ~ ½ cup
Chicken ~ 5-6 pieces, the less fleshy parts used to make stock
Salt ~ to taste

Cook the rice with the rest of the ingredients till cooked well. Remove the chicken pieces from the rice and serve hot.

couscous cochin

Malabari Jews, Ilanit Menachem

Couscous was never a part of Kerala cuisine.This recipe emerged within the Kerala-Jewish community in Israel, after the diaspora. Created by the Cochinni Jews in Israel, the couscous found a new preparation with Kerala ingredients. The original version calls for the use of semolina and can be used as a substitute for rice or bread

Couscous ~ 3 cups
Turmeric powder ~ ½ tsp
Onion ~ 1 large, chopped
Black mustard seeds ~ 1 tsp
Curry leaves ~ 1 small bunch
Water ~ 4 cups
Salt ~ to taste
Oil ~ 6 tbsp

Heat the oil in a pan and fry the onions till they change colour. Add the curry leaves and the mustard seeds. Now, add the spices and the salt. Add the water and when it boils add the couscous. Cook till the water dries up. Break the couscous with a fork and cover the pot with a lid.

COMMON STAPLES WITH RICE AND BREAD

Some staples are universal, and it is difficult to limit them to specific communities. Influences may have come from varied sources. Idiyappam, for example, is also seen in Sri Lanka which has a strong Dutch influence

ariputtu

STEAMED RICE CAKE

Syrian Christian, Sarala Thomas Palivathukkal

It is said the Portuguese invented the puttu, an easy staple for their travels on boats and ships, which later became a popular food across Kerala. Puttu was originally made in bamboo steamers or coconut shells made for the purpose. Now, more practical and user-friendly metal puttu-makers are available. Previously, rice was powdered using a granite tool called oralu and a heavy wooden cylindrical hand-operated pounder, crushing the grains to a fine texture. Later, mills were set up which ground the rice. Today, ready-to-use rice powder is available in the market

Rice powder ~ 1 cup, roasted
Grated coconut ~ ½ cup
Water ~ to moisten
Salt ~ to taste

Sieve the rice flour and place in a dish. Add the salt and the water gradually, mixing the rice powder with fingers to remove any clumps.

Sieve the mixture to obtain a fine powder (the mixture must be moist enough but not clumpy).

Add a portion of the coconut. Heat water to steam in the puttukodam or pot.

To the puttukuti or the steamer, add a layer of the shredded coconut and top it up with the rice powder mixture, adding some more coconut in the end. Close the puttukutti and place on the puttukodam to steam.

Let the puttu cook for about 10-12 minutes. Using a wooden rod push the cooked puttu out of the kutti on to a serving plate.

Serve hot.

maniputtu

Latin Catholic, Annie Burleigh

Similar to Ariputtu, Maniputtu is made from small balls of the rice flour, where 'mani' means 'tiny bell' in Malayalam. Often eaten with sweetened coconut milk

Rice flour ~ 1 cup
Coconut ~ 1 cup, grated
Oil ~ ½ tsp
Water ~ 3/4 cup
Salt ~ to taste

Heat water in a vessel with salt. When it boils, add the rice flour and mix well. Remove from fire to cool. When still warm, knead well. Oil palms and make small balls of the dough. Heat water in the puttukodam. Layer the puttukutti with the rice balls and coconut alternatively in a 4:1 proportion. Place the kutti on the kodam and steam till cooked.

kallappam

BREAD MADE USING TODDY

Syrian Christian, Sarla Thomas Palivathukkal

The same batter can be used to make Valliappam or Lace Hoppers. Valliappam is made in an appachatti, a shallow utensil that offers a lace edge to the bread. Kallappam is flat bread, the batter spread on a hot iron griddle to cook

Raw rice ~ 1 cup
Parboiled rice ~ ½ cup
Grated coconut ~ 1 cup
Sugar ~ 2-3 tsp
Kallu/toddy ~ ½ cup
Water ~ to soak rice
Salt ~ to taste

Soak the raw rice overnight. Grind all the ingredients together except toddy to make a mix of semi-fine pourable consistency.

Add the toddy and the salt and let it ferment for 8-10 hours. Once it ferments and rises, pour a ladleful on a hot griddle and cook over medium flame, turning it when required.

idiyappam

STRING HOPPERS

Syrian Christian, Mary Mathew Madathikunnel

Idiyappam is eaten with curry or along with sweetened, thick coconut milk. To make the milk, add a little flour in it along with sugar and heat on low flame till the sauce thickens but is of pourable consistency

Rice flour ~ 1 cup

Water ~ 1 to 1½ cups (water depends on the quality of the rice flour)

Salt ~ to taste

Oil ~ 2 tsp

Coconut ~ 2 tbsp, shredded

Boil water with the oil and salt. Add the water to the flour in a thick stream, mixing the flour with a fork. Knead and then allow it to cool for 2 minutes. Oil the palms to avoid the dough from sticking.

Rub a little oil on the moulds of an idiyappam maker. Sprinkle the coconut in them, and using the idiyappam maker, take a small portion of the dough, place it inside the press and press it down, allowing the idiyappam strands to emerge from the other end.

In a circular motion, fill the moulds with the strands, tapering off as the layer. Once all the moulds are filled, steam on medium to high flame for five minutes or until cooked. Serve hot.

choru

BOILED RICE

Syrian Christian, Sarla Thomas Palivathukkal

Kerala rice refers to unpolished raw rice. Kanji is also a staple popularly eaten in Kerala, which is the gruel before the water is drained from the rice. Kanji requires more cooking and the rice is of a very soft consistency. The starchy water was used to starch cotton in days of yore

Raw (Kerala) rice ~ 1 cup
Water ~ 3-4 cups

Wash and clean the raw rice. Cook in a pressure cooker until well done. Drain the water in a colander and serve hot.

matzah bread

PARADESI JEW, SARAH COHEN

Syrian Christian, Sarla Thomas Palivathukkal

An unleavened bread made during Passover. It is now rarely made

Wheat flour
Water ~ ¼ cup, add or lessen flour as needed
Salt ~ as required
Oil ~ Sufficient to make the flour dough supple

Mix the flour with salt, oil, and the water to get a soft dough. Sprinkle some more flour on a rolling board and roll out balls about the size of a cricket ball. This is the measurement Sarah used. Grill on a hot pan, turning it frequently. Bread should be brown and crisp.

MEATS AND FISH

Meen moilee prepared in Latin Catholic style uses coriander powder and potatoes, offering a different flavour from the Syrian version. My grandmother used to add macaroni to the dish, a preparation created and popular in Fort Kochi

meen moilee

FISH MOLEE

Latin Catholic, Annie Burleigh Kurishingal

Fish ~ 1 kg, medium pieces
Coconut ~ 1, (first and second milk)
Turmeric powder ~ 1 tsp
Coriander powder ~ 2 tsp
Onions ~ 2, cubed into four
Ginger ~ 1 inch, sliced fine
Green chillies ~ 6
Shallots ~ 6, whole
Cinnamon ~ 1, 2" stick
Cloves ~ 3
Peppercorns ~ 4
Potatoes ~ 2, cubed into four, parboiled
Vinegar ~ 1 tsp or as required
Salt ~ to taste
Dalda or oil ~ 1 tbsp

Heat the dalda and fry the shallots over medium flame. Add the spice powders, and the green chillies followed by the second milk of the coconut, the potatoes, fish pieces, the onions and the other spices, vinegar and salt. Cook on low flame till the fish is done. Add the first milk and switch the flame off once it begins to boil.

meen moilee

FISH MOLEE

Syrian Christian, Mary Mathew Madathikunnal

A popular fish preparation, the molee or moilee is mainly eaten with appam. Shrimp can be used instead of fish

1. Fish ~ 4 slices
   Salt ~ 1 tsp
   Chilli powder ~ ½ tsp
   Turmeric powder ~ 1 tsp
   Marinate the fish and keep for a few minutes. After that lightly fry the fish
2. Green chillies ~ 4
   Onion ~ 1, sliced fine
   Ginger ~ inch, sliced, fine
   Garlic ~ 3, sliced
   Pepper ~ 1 tsp, crushed
   Curry leaves ~ 3-4
   Coconut milk of one coconut ~ first, second and third milk
   Coconut oil ~ 2-3 tbsp
   Salt ~ to taste
   Vinegar ~ 1 tsp or as required

Make a paste of all ingredients in (1) and apply to the fish pieces. In a shallow pan, heat oil and fry over low flame. Avoid over frying.

In a pan, add the coconut oil and when it gets heated, add ginger and garlic.

To this, add the sliced onions and chillies. When it turns soft add green chillies, curry leaves, pepper, salt and third milk.

When it boils add the fish slices and the second milk and vinegar. When gravy thickens (after approximately 5 minutes), add the first milk. Lower the flame and allow it to simmer for about a minute, then remove from fire.

meen pal curry

FISH WITH GREEN MANGOES AND COCONUT MILK

Syrian Christian, Sarala Thomas Pallivathukal

A popular preparation, the recipe changes slightly from region to region in Kerala. This is the Syrian Christian version using green mangoes, followed by the Latin Catholic version, which is the next recipe. Both use coconut milk but the sour ingredient may differ regionally. Best eaten with rice

Fish ~ 1 kg, sliced
Green mango ~ 1 large, sliced
Green chillies ~ 4
Ginger ~ 1" long, sliced
Red chilli powder ~ 3 tsp
Turmeric powder ~ 1 tsp
Garlic ~ 3-4 cloves, sliced
Onions ~ 1 large, sliced
Coconut milk ~ 1 coconut, first and second milk
Coconut oil ~ 2 tbsp
Vinegar ~ if required, based on the sourness of the green mango
Salt ~ to taste

Make a paste of the red chilli and turmeric powders with a little water. In a pan, sauté the onions, garlic, ginger and green chillies. Now, add the paste and continue sautéing till cooked.

Add the second coconut milk, mango slices, salt and vinegar. Add the fish and lower the flame. Once the fish is cooked, add the first milk.

Allow one boil and turn off the flame. Garnish with curry leaves.

meen pal curry

FISH CURRY IN COCONUT MILK

Latin Catholic, Annie Burleigh

Bilimbipuli (referred to and known as green tamarind) is a delicious option to vinegar. It may be used in this recipe instead of vinegar

Fish (pomfret or mullet) ~ four, medium size
Coriander powder ~ 1½ tbsp
Red chilli powder ~ ½ tbsp
Turmeric powder ~ ½ tbsp
Shallots (medium size) ~ 20, crushed
Ginger ~ 1½ pieces
Green chillies ~ 3, diced
Curry leaves ~ one small bunch
Vinegar and salt ~ to taste
Coconut milk ~ 1 small coconut, first and second milk

Grind the coriander powder, chilli powder, and turmeric powder together with a little water to make a thick paste.

Heat the oil in a deep pan and sauté the shallots till soft. Add the ground spices till the oil rises above. Add the curry leaves, ginger and green chillies.

Lower the flame and add the second milk of the coconut.

Bring this to a boil and add the vinegar, the fish and salt. Cook till fish is done.

Lower the flame and add the first milk and allow the gravy to lightly boil for a few seconds. Remove from flame and serve hot.

meen pacha manga curry

FISH WITH GREEN MANGO

Malabari Jews, Ilanit Menachem

Use of black pepper in this recipe is unique to the Jews of Cochin. No coconut milk is used either

1. Mullet ~ 1-2, sliced
   Black pepper ~ ½ tsp
   Salt ~ ¾ tsp
   Turmeric ~ 1 tsp
   Red chilli powder ~ 1 tsp
   Coriander powder ~ 1 tsp
   Water ~ 1-2 tbsp, as required
   Oil ~ for frying

2. Green (raw) mango ~ 1, sliced
   Coriander leaves ~ 1 bunch
   Curry leaves ~ a handful
   Peppercorns ~ 3
   Garlic cloves ~ 3
   Water ~ 1 cup
   Black pepper powder ~ ½ tsp
   Red chilli powder ~ 1 tsp
   Turmeric powder ~ ½ tsp
   Coriander powder ~ 1 tsp
   Tamarind ~ 1 tbsp
   Tomato paste ~ 3 tbsp
   Water ~ 1 cup

1. Make a paste of all the ingredients and rub the fish with it generously. Keep in the refrigerator for half an hour. Heat oil in a pan and fry the fish slices. Keep aside.

Grind all the ingredients in set 2 together. Keep the tomato paste aside.

Heat oil in a pan and add the tomatoes. Sauté for a few minutes and add the water. Once the water begins to boil, add the spices and the ground mixture along with the fried fish.

Let it cook on medium flame till the water evaporates and the sauce coats the fish. Garnish with curry leaves or coriander leaves.

meen pollichathu

FISH IN BANANA LEAF

Latin Catholic, Annie Burleigh

This version is unique to Fort Kochi. The use of coconut milk and the omission of many spices change it from the spicier Syrian recipe

Fish (preferably mullet) ~ 1, cleaned and slit
Chilli powder ~ ½ tsp
Turmeric powder ~ ¼ tsp
Peppercorns ~ 8
Coconut milk ~ ½ coconut and its first milk
Shallots ~ 12
Green chillies ~ 2
Banana leaves ~ for wrapping
Oil ~ ¼ tsp
Salt ~ to taste
Water ~ to make a thick paste

Marinate the fish with a paste of chilli powder, turmeric powder, 3 peppercorns, salt and water. Grind all the remaining ingredients and keep aside.

Over a low flame tenderise a banana leaf by heating the leaf on both sides. When cool, oil the leaf.

Place a layer of the ground paste on the oiled banana leaf. Place the fish and add the remaining paste. Wrap the fish in the banana leaf and tie with a string.

Place the wrapped fish on a hot griddle and cook on medium flame, turning it occasionally. Serve hot without opening the banana wrapping.

karimeen elayil pollichathu

FISH IN BANANA LEAF

Syrian Christian, Parayil family

The original recipe calls for the fish masala to be simmered dry over coal and then applied to the fish

Karimeen (Pearl spot) ~ 1 kg
Shallots ~ 250 gm, finely minced
Green chillies ~ 8, sliced
Ginger ~ 2 pieces, sliced
Garlic ~ 20 flakes, sliced
Tomatoes ~ 3, finely chopped
Chilli powder ~ 3 tbsp
Coconut oil ~ 150 ml
Salt ~ to taste
Banana leaves ~ for wrapping

Clean the fish and make gnashes on them. Keep aside a teaspoon of oil.

Mix the remaining ingredients in the rest of the oil. Line a *meenchatti* (or a pan for cooking fish) with four layers of banana leaves.

Spread the rest of the oil and half of the spice paste on the last banana leaf. Arrange the fish slices on the leaf, spread the remaining spices on them and cover with a lid. Cook on low flame and wait for it to boil.

Cook over coal or in an oven till the gravy dries up and the onions are browned, being careful that it does not stick to the bottom of the pan. Once the spice paste is fairly dry and cooked, switch the flame off.

Serve the fish wrapped in the banana leaves.

meen chuttathu

FISH BARBEQUE

Syrian Christian, Parayil family

Chuttathu refers to having been cooked over coal. Kodumpulli needs to be soaked for about 15 minutes to half an hour for the sourness and flavour to seep into the water. Eaten during a meal or even as a snack

Karimeen (Pearl spot) ~ 1 kg
Coconut oil ~ ¾ cup
Red chillies deseeded and soaked
Shallots ~ 200 gm
Garlic ~ 4 flakes
Ginger ~ 1 inch
Kodumpulli[1] ~ 1
Vinegar or water in which kodumpulli is soaked
Salt ~ to taste

Grind all ingredients except the fish and sauté well in oil. Once the mixed spices change colour and an aroma rises, place the fish in it. Wrap the fish pieces in banana leaves and cook over coal or in an oven.

1 **Kodumpulli** – *Garcinia cambogia,* or 'Malabar Tamarind' (also called brindleberry) is found in tropical countries. The ripe fruit is halved or sectioned and spread out in thin layers, dried in the sun and smoked. Common salt is added during drying. The fruits are acidic and are also eaten raw or pickled. The fleshy rind and extracts, fresh or after drying and smoking, are used as a condiment and flavouring in many traditional curries, especially fish curries. Also used as a substitute for tamarind, mango and lime.

nenmeen curry

WHITE POMFRET CURRY

Syrian Christian, Parayil family

This recipe specifically calls for white pomfret. Some versions omit peppercorns

Nenmeen ~ 1.5 kg
Milk from half a coconut
Onions ~ 3, large
Green chillies ~ 4
Ginger ~ 2, one small piece sliced, one larger piece to grind
Garlic ~ 5 flakes
Peppercorns ~ 20
Turmeric ~ ½ tsp
White vinegar ~ 1 tbsp
Salt ~ to taste
Oil ~ 1-2 tbsp
Water ~ ¼ cup

Grind the peppercorns, ginger, garlic, and turmeric. Reserve a teaspoon of the spices and smear the fish with the remaining paste.

Heat a little oil and sauté the onions, green chillies and ginger. When done, add the fish. Add the water to the reserved spice paste and pour over the fish.

Add the salt and allow it to cook on low flame.

Once the fish is done, add the vinegar and the coconut milk. Simmer till the gravy is fairly thick.

chemeen eerkalayil kuthiyethu

PRAWNS IN BROOMSTICK SKEWERS

Syrian Christian, Parayil family

A pan fried preparation, the masala takes an interesting flavour when cooked in oil. Ensure the flame is low to prevent the spices from burning

Tiger prawns ~ 1 kg
Kashmiri chilli ~ 8
Garlic ~ 8 flakes
Peppercorns ~ ½ tsp
Cumin seeds ~ 1 pinch
Coriander seeds ~ 10 gm
Sugar ~ A pinch
Turmeric ~ 1 tsp
Puli (tamarind) ~ 5 gm
Salt ~ to taste

Grind with a little water all ingredients except the prawns and keep aside. Slit the prawns from the inner side lengthwise. Stuff each prawn with the ground spices. Pierce a freshly skinned broomstick or skewer through the back of the prawns, just below the head and to the tail. Let it marinate for about half an hour. Heat the oil and shallow fry, turning the skewer from time to time.

onaka chemeen (I)

DRY PRAWN FRY

Syrian Christian, *Mary Mathew Madathikunnel*

A perfect condiment with rice and curry, kanji, even as a snack with drinks

Dry prawn ~ 1 cup (head and tail removed)
Onion ~ 1 big, chopped
Coconut oil ~ 2 tbsp
Chilli powder ~ 1½ tsp
Curry leaves ~ 4-5
Salt ~ to taste

Wash the dry prawns and strain it in a sieve, allowing the water to drain out. Place a deep pan on the fire and heat it over a medium flame.

Now, add the prawns and stir it till all the water evaporates and the prawns are dry. Add the oil, onions, curry leaves, and salt. Fry until the onions turn golden brown and the prawn is crispy. Reduce the flame and add chilli powder and stir till its raw smell leaves.

Remove from fire. Cool and store in a glass bottle.

njandu curry

CRAB CURRY

Malabar Mappila, Rasheeda and Rahima Meethalakath

This curry is best eaten with rice. Coriander leaves can be substituted with curry leaves, if desired

Crab ~ ½ kg, cleaned and pieced
Onion ~ 1
Tomato ~ 1
Ginger paste ~ 1 tsp
Garlic paste ~ 1 tsp
Chilli powder ~ 1 tsp
Coriander powder ~ 1 tsp
Turmeric powder ~ ½ tsp
Coconut ~ ½, grated
Cumin ~ 1 tsp
Shallots ~ 4
Oil ~ 2 tsp

Cook the crab in sufficient water for gravy along with the salt. Grind with a little water the grated coconut, with the cumin, coriander powder, chilli powder and turmeric powder to a paste. Heat the oil in a pan and sauté the paste. Add this to the cooked crab and sprinkle coriander leaves. Cook till the gravy slightly thickens.

fish kofta curry

Paradesi Jews, Queenie Hallegua

Kofta is a Middle Eastern dish made usually of meat. This is a fish version; valanpuli and other local spices make the recipe completely different from regular kofta recipes

Fish fillet ~ 250 gm
Onion ~ 5, sliced
Chilli powder ~ 3 tbsp
Coriander powder ~ 1 heaped tbsp
Valanpuli (fresh tamarind) ~ the size of a small egg
Oil ~ ½ cup
Turmeric powder ~ 2 tsp
Garlic ~ 1 big pod
Ginger ~ 2''
Green chillies ~ slit, 6
Curry leaves ~ 5
Celery ~ 2 sticks
Sugar ~ 1 tbsp

~

Mince the fish using a mincer.

Slice four of the onions, apply a little salt and keep aside. Squeeze out the water from the onions and mince them. Chop celery and add it along with the onions to the fish. Add one tsp of the turmeric powder, one tablespoon of oil and salt to taste. Mix well and form small kofta balls.

For the gravy, grind the chilli powder, coriander powder, garlic, ginger and turmeric with a little water to a fine paste.

With one cup of water, extract the juice from the tamarind (valanpuli).

Slice remaining onions and fry in oil along with green chillies and curry leaves. Add the spice paste and fry well. Next add the tamarind water, a cup of water, sugar and salt. Add the kofta balls to the gravy. Stir by gently shifting the vessel with hands. Allow the gravy to thicken.

Celery can be replaced with mint or coriander. Leftovers of this dish are also baked for the next day.

Another version is to fry the fish kofta balls before adding them to the gravy.

chemeen ularthu

SHRIMP DRY FRY

Latin Catholic, Annie Burleigh

This recipe of the ularthu is an easy item to make, strikingly different from and a less tangy version of the Syrian Christian recipe of meen chuttathu cooked with karimeen, although many of the ingredients are common and the cooking processes bear similarity. However the shrimp ularthu does not use kodumpulli (Malabar tamarind) or coconut. Adding browned onions as a garnish adds to the flavour

Shrimp, cleaned and deveined ~ ¾ kg
Shallots ~ 10
Chilli powder ~ ½ tsp
Green chillies ~ 2, slit
Oil ~ 1 tablespoon
Salt ~ to taste
Water ~ to sprinkle

In a pan, heat the oil and sauté the shallots. When they turn colour, add the chilli powder and green chillies. Add the shrimp and the salt. Sprinkle with a little water and cook till the shrimp is tender.

challam porichathu

SPICED PRAWN PATTIES

Latin Catholic, Annie Burleigh

A unique form of prawn cutlets, they work best with fresh prawns. Also made in Anglo-Indian homes

Prawn ~ ¼ tsp
Pepper ~ ½ tsp
Cumin ~ ½ tsp
Garlic ~ 1 small pod
Red chilli powder ~ one pinch
Green chilli ~ 1
Shallots ~ 2
Salt ~ to taste

Grind all of the above ingredients and make them into flat, circular rounds. Heat oil in a pan and fry till golden brown to serve hot.

fish mustard curry

Anglo-Indian, Howard La'frenais

Mustard adds the punch to this curry; it is best eaten with rice

1. Baby shark or skate ~ 1 kg
Coconut ~ ½, first and second milk
Oil ~ half cup
Prepared [husked] mustard to sprinkle
Vinegar ~ to taste
Salt ~ to taste
2. Chilli powder ~ 4 tbsp
Saffron powder ~ 1 tbsp
Mustard seeds ~ 2 tbsp
Ginger ~ one, 2" long
Garlic cloves ~ 8
Small cumin ~ 1 tsp
Shallots ~ 15, sliced
Green chillies ~ 3, slit

Grind together the ingredients in set 2.

Heat oil in a shallow dish and sauté onions, green chillies, sliced ginger. Add the ground masala and when cooked well, add the second milk, vinegar and salt. Add the fish pieces.

When the fish is cooked, add the first milk, the husked mustard and bring the curry to a simmer.

Take the pan off the flame and serve the dish hot.

choragu curry

BABY SHARK CURRY

Latin Catholic, Annie Burleigh

Baby shark alone is to be used, the frying of the ground mixture of spices is what offers the special flavour

1. Baby shark ~ 1½ kg, sliced
   Fish tamarind ~ 1-2 soaked in water
   Shallots ~ 10
   Garlic ~ 2 small pods, sliced
   Ginger ~ 1 finger long, sliced
   Red chilli powder ~ 1 tsp
   Turmeric powder ~ 1 tsp
2. Grated half coconut
   Coriander powder ~ 1 tsp
   Pepper powder ~ ½ tsp
   Red chilli powder ~ 1 tsp
   Cumin ~ 1 tsp
   Curry leaves ~ 3-4 leaves
   Oil ~ 3 tbsp

Place the fish (shark) slices along with the rest of the ingredients in set 1 and cook till done. Grind the ingredients in set 2 together, except curry leaves. In a shallow pan, heat oil and fry the ground mixture. Add the curry leaves and sauté well. Add the mixture to the fish curry. Serve with rice.

chala curry

SARDINE CURRY

Malabari Jews, Ilanit Menachem

The common man's curry, is a version made by the Jews of Kerala. The original version is a spicy curry with raw mango or kodumpulli

Sardines ~ 1 kg, cleaned
Turmeric powder ~ ½ tsp
Coriander powder ~ ½ tsp
Salt ~ to taste
Oil ~ ½ cup
Onions ~ 1, sliced
Garlic cloves ~ 5, sliced
Curry leaves ~ a handful
Dry red chilli ~ 3, chopped
Black mustard seeds ~ 1 tsp
Tomato paste ~ 3 tbsp
Sugar ~ 2 tbsp
Vinegar ~ ⅓ cup
Red chilli powder ~ 1 tsp
Turmeric powder ~ 1 tsp
Coriander powder ~ 1 tsp
Salt ~ to taste
Water ~ 1½ cups

Make a paste of the turmeric and coriander powders with water, add a little salt to it. Rub the sardines generously inside out with the paste. Heat oil in a deep pan and fry till brown.

Add the mustard seeds and when it splutters add onions and once it turns colour add the dry chillies. Add the spices, tomato paste and vinegar.

Add the water and bring it to a boil.

Cook for 5-10 minutes and then add the fried fish. Allow it to simmer till the gravy thickens and coats the fish.

Garnish with fresh curry leaves.

marak

FISH BALL SOUP

Paradesi Jews,
Queenie Hallegua

Marak refers to soup. Fish can be replaced with chicken to which celery or mint leaves may be added instead of coriander. This dish accompanied with rice formed the first proper meal fed to Jewish babies

for the fish balls

Fish ~ 250 gm
Onions ~ 4 medium size
Turmeric powder ~ 1 tsp
Oil ~ 2 tbsp.
Salt ~ to taste
Coriander leaves ~ 1 bunch

for the gravy

Onion ~ 1
Potato ~ 1 large, cubed small
Carrot ~ 1 large, cubed small
Tomato ~ 1 large, cubed small
Oil ~ 3 tbsp
Turmeric ~ 1 tsp
Coriander ~ 1 bunch
Salt ~ to taste
Water ~ 3 cups

To make the balls, mince the fish and keep it aside. Now, mince the onions along with the salt. Keep quarter portion of it aside and squeeze out the water from the remaining minced onions. Discard the water. Add the fish to the onions along with chopped coriander leaves and turmeric and oil. Mix well and shape into lime size balls.

For the gravy, slice all the vegetables and place in a pan with the water. Add the turmeric, oil and salt and boil till the vegetables are soft. Strain the liquid and keep aside. Puree the vegetables and add it to the liquid, allow it to boil once again. Once of a gravy consistency, add the fish balls and cook for five minutes. Sprinkle fresh coriander leaves before serving.

tuna pastel

Paradesi Jews, Sarah Cohen

A very popular snack amongst Cochinni Jews, the contents of the pastel can be varied. Pastel or pasthel in Cochin is different from elsewhere because of the locally available ingredients. Late Sara Cohen shared this recipe before she passed away in August 2019, leaving just two more Paradesi Jews in Kochi and India. Sarah's memory recalls this snack being served on Friday evenings at the home of Queenie Hallegua's parents, an open-house event every week for friends and family

Tuna ~ 1 tin/or its equivalent of fresh tuna
Onion ~ 1 large, diced
Tomatoes ~ 1 large, diced
Green chillies ~ 2, diced
Coriander leaves ~ one small bunch, chopped
Rice flour ~ 1 cup
Flour ~ ¼ cup
Eggs ~ 2
Oil ~ 1 tbsp

Drain oil from the tin and heat in a saucepan. Add the onions and chillies and fry till light brown. Add tomatoes and sauté till cooked. Add the tuna and salt and mix well.

Add the coriander leaves last and mix well.

for the dough

Sieve the rice flour and flour into a vessel. Add the eggs and enough water to make a thin, clear batter. Add salt and oil and mix well.

Heat a saucepan and pour a small amount of the batter into it. Swirl and pour out the excess to form a thin coating. Cook till the edges start peeling off from the pan. Remove from pan and fill with the tuna filling, keeping the edges free.

Fold the edges on both sides and roll up till the filling is completely enclosed. Heat oil in a vessel and fry till brown.

meen acharu

FISH PICKLE

Syrian Christian, Parayil family

A Christian preparation, meen acharu is a favourite pickle eaten with rice

Any fleshy fish ~ 1 kg, cut into small chunks
Green chillies ~ 10
Garlic ~ ½ cup
Ginger ~ 1 tbsp, sliced
Oil (vegetable or gingelly) ~ ½ cup
Vinegar ~ 1 cup
Dry red chillies ~ 10
Turmeric ~ 1 tsp
Peppercorns ~ 1 tsp
Mustard ~ 1 tsp
Fenugreek ~ 1 tsp
Curry leaves ~ A few
Salt ~ to taste

Marinate the fish in a paste made of two teaspoons chilli powder, one-teaspoon turmeric powder, water and salt to taste.

Grind in about two tablespoons of vinegar the fenugreek, dry red chillies, turmeric and pepper. Heat the oil and fry the fish, keep aside.

Fry the green chillies, garlic and ginger and remove from the oil. Now, splutter the mustard in the oil and add the ground paste.

When cooked, add the remaining vinegar, salt and the fried fish. Simmer for about five minutes.

When cool, store in a clean glass jar.

chemeen pada

SHRIMP PICKLE

Latin Catholic, Annie Burleigh

A pickle popular in my family, Pada reminisces the Portuguese tradition of pickling meats in vinegar, paprika and salt for their long sea voyages. Pada has a short shelf life if left outside. Refrigerate for long-term use. Best tasting when eaten fresh and without refrigeration.This recipe is a speciality of my grandmother's kitchen

Prawns ~ 1½ kg, medium size
Garlic ~ 4 pods, large size
Cumin seeds ~ 2 tbsp
Chilli powder (less pungent) ~ 4 tbsp
Turmeric powder ~ 1½ tsp
Vinegar ~ as required
Salt ~ to taste
Oil ~ for frying

Marinate the prawns in turmeric powder and salt. In a deep- bottom pan, deep fry well and keep aside.

Grind the remaining ingredients together in vinegar. Strain the oil in which the prawns were fried and use to sauté the ground spices till the oil rises to the top.

Add the prawns, vinegar and salt and allow the pickle to boil.

Cool and pour into dry glass jars.

onaka chemeen (II)

DRIED SHRIMP

Syrian Christian, Mary Mathew Madathikunnel

This is a great accompaniment to rice and can be used instead of pickles. Its shelf life is long and it can stay for months

Dried shrimp ~ 1 cup
Crushed red chilli flakes ~ ½ tbsp
Shallots, crushed ~ 25
Curry leaves ~ 4-5
Oil ~ 1½ tbsp

Wash the shrimps and dry well. In a pan, dry roast the shrimps on low heat. Heat oil on medium flame in a shallow vessel and fry the shallots to brown. Reduce the heat and add the curry leaves, crushed chilli, and the dried shrimp.

Mix well. When the shrimp changes colour to a deep reddish-brown, remove from fire. When cool, store in a glass jar.

folitz'zh

FISH IN SPICY GRAVY

Malabari Jews, Ilanit Menachem

A take on the fish pollichathu, this is a milder version of it. Green chilli and red chilli powder can be increased to add fire to the flavour. Some cook the fish further in a banana leaf where the gravy coats the fish well

Fish ~ fillet, sliced
Garlic ~ 2, diced fine
Green chilli ~ 1, sliced fine
Curry leaves ~ 1 small bunch
Tomato puree ~ 4 tbsp
Turmeric powder ~ ½ tsp
Red chilli powder ~ 1 tsp
Coriander powder ~ ½ tsp
Ginger paste ~ 1 tsp
Tamarind ~ 1 tsp
Oil ~ As needed

Make a paste of the spices with a little oil and rub it generously over the fish slices. Refrigerate for half an hour and fry in hot oil. Keep the fish aside.

Take some of the oil in which the fish was fried, and in another pan fry the onions, garlic and curry leaves. Add the tomato puree, the tamarind and salt and sauté well.

Add the fish slices and on low heat cook till the sauce coats the fish well.

Garnish with fresh curry leaves.

prawn balcham

Anglo-Indian, Howard La'frenais

Not to be confused with the Goan balchao, this version used bilimbipuli that offers a unique sourness to the dish. Similar to the Syrian Christian fish curry, this dish has a tangy flavour

1. Prawns ~ 100
   Bilimbipuli ~ 2 fistfuls, sliced
   Ginger ~ 2 pieces, chopped
   Green chillies ~ 10, chopped fine
   Coconut oil ~ 3 tbsp
   Salt ~ to taste
   Water ~ to cook
2. Red chilli powder ~ 1 tbsp
   Small cumin seeds ~ 1 tsp
   Garlic cloves ~ 5
   Turmeric ~ 1 tsp

Grind together the ingredients under set 2.

Cook the prawns with just enough water to cover them, along with ½ tsp salt. When done, drain the prawns and grind coarsely. In the drained water, boil the bilimbipuli, green chillies, ginger and ground masala. When the bilimbipuli is cooked, add the prawns. Temper with coconut oil when done.

duck baffad

Anglo-Indian, Howard La'frenais

My grandmother often cooked pork baffad. The flavour is unique and light; what stood out were turmeric, pepper and coriander. Duck baffad is equally flavourful

1. Duck ~ 1, cut into pieces
   Potatoes ~ ½ kg
   Vinegar ~ 2 tbsp.
   Salt ~ to taste
   Ghee ~ 4 tbsp
   Water ~ 3 cups
   Onions ~ 3, sliced
   Green chillies ~ 6, sliced
   Garlic ~ 6
   Ginger ~ 1, 2" piece
2. Dry chillies ~ 8
   Coriander seeds ~ 2 tbsp
   Peppercorns ~ 10
   Turmeric ~ 1" long
   Cloves ~ 6
   Cinnamon ~ 2 pieces

Grind together the ingredients under set 2.

Cut and wash the duck. In a pot, mix the duck with the ground masala, vinegar, salt and water. Cook till done.

Add the potatoes and the sliced ingredients along with ghee. Simmer till the gravy is fairly thick and the potatoes are done.

kozhi kurumulagu

PEPPER CHICKEN

Syrian Christian, Parayil family

An easy to prepare recipe, the flavour of pepper stands out distinctly but is balanced with the presence of the other spices

Chicken ~ 1.5 kg, pieces
Pepper ~ 10 gm
Perumjeerakam (black cumin seeds or shah jeera) ~ 10 gm
Ginger ~ 10 gm
Garlic ~ 10 gm
Green chilli ~ 3
Onions ~ 3 medium sized, sliced
Cloves ~ 4

Add the remaining ingredients and cook till the meat is tender and the spice paste has coated the chicken well.

madhura-kizhangu kozhi stew

SWEET POTATO AND RICE CHICKEN STEW

Malabari Jews, Ilanit Menachem

This dish can be made without chicken and eggs, and served as a vegetarian meal as well. The dish was served in Cochin on Fridays for supper; when served on a Saturday, it was called Foto'o

Chicken ~ ½ cup, diced
Onions ~ 2, sliced
Garlic ~ 3 cloves
Rice ~ ¾ cup
Sweet potato ~ 2, cut into cubes
Plantain ~ 1, sliced into cubes
Coconut ~ ½ cup, shredded
Brown sugar ~ 2 tbsp
Vinegar ~ 1 tbsp
Water ~ 2 cups
Eggs ~ Boiled, one per person
Salt ~ to taste
Oil ~ 1 tbsp

Heat the oil and fry a slice of onion. Add the chicken and fry till brown. Add the sweet potato, plantain and the rice. Add water, salt and vinegar. Let it cook.

Grind together the garlic, onion, and coconut with a little water. Add this to the rice mixture and cook on low flame for 45 minutes. Transfer the contents to a dish and bake in a preheated oven for 20 minutes.

Place the boiled eggs on the cooked dish and serve.

nadan kozhi curry

COUNTRY CHICKEN CURRY

Syrian Christian, *Mary Mathew Madathikunnel*

This is a common chicken curry found in most Kerala homes. The flavour may differ slightly from one kitchen to another, simply because of the change of a few ingredients. Adding coconut milk to the curry is yet another option

Chicken ~ 1.5 to 2 kg (Curry cut/ small pieces)
Onions ~ 4, sliced
Curry leaves ~ 1 stem
Ginger ~ 1 tbsp, ground
Garlic ~ 1 tbsp, ground
Green chillies ~ 3, slit
Chilli powder ~ 2 tbsp
Pepper powder ~ 1 tsp
Turmeric powder ~ ½ tsp
Coriander powder ~ 3 tbsp
Garam masala ~ 1 tsp, heaped
Tomato ~ 2, cubed, small
Coconut oil ~ 4 tbsp
Salt ~ to taste
Water ~ to cook the chicken

Heat the coconut oil in a pan. Add the ginger and garlic pastes. Sauté well on medium flame. Now, add the sliced onion along with the salt.

Continue to sauté until the onion is cooked well. Add the curry leaves, chilli, coriander, turmeric powders and sauté well. Once cooked well, add the pepper and garam masala powder, sauté well by adding a little water (about a teaspoon) until the oil rises on top.

Now, add the chicken pieces and allow the masala to coat them, mixing the pieces constantly.

Add enough water to obtain a thick gravy. Cover and let the meat cook well. Check for salt.

When the chicken is done remove from fire.

onaki vevichathu

MINTY CARROT CHICKEN

Paradesi Jews, Queenie Hallegua

This dish is a combination of mint and spices. Carrots can be replaced with gourd, potatoes, cauliflower or beans. A version of the curry also uses ginger and garlic, along with a few green chillies for spice

Carrots ~ 600 gm, sliced fine
Onions ~ 3 large, sliced
Chicken ~ 1, medium sized pieces
Turmeric ~ 1 tsp
Mint leaves ~ One bunch
Oil ~ ½ cup
Salt ~ to taste

Heat oil in a vessel and fry onions till they turn brown. Add turmeric powder and then the chicken pieces and sauté well. Add water to cover the chicken and the salt and cook over low flame.

When half done, add carrots. Cook till meat and carrots are done and all the water dries up. Garnish with mint leaves. The mint offers a fine flavour to an indigenous dish. It is commonly served with rice or bread.

chicken with tomato and rice

Malabari Jews, Ilanit Menachem

Eaten as a preparation on its own, this recipe is a quick fix meal

Rice ~ 2 cups
Chicken legs ~ 6 pieces
Onion ~ 1, diced
Tomatoes (juicy and soft) ~ 5, diced
Eggs ~ Boiled, one per person
Black pepper ~ 5 corns
Turmeric powder ~ ½ tsp
Salt ~ to taste
Oil ~ 2 tbsp
Water ~ 4 cups

Heat the oil and fry the onions till they turn translucent. Add the diced tomatoes and the chicken.

Add the spices and water and cook for half an hour. Add the rice and cook till water and the juices evaporate partially and the rice is partly (¾) cooked.

Remove from the heat and arrange the eggs on the rice. Cook in the oven at 100 degrees for 2 hours.

Serve hot.

pollichaze

CORIANDER FRIED CHICKEN

Paradesi Jews, Queenie Hallegua

The coriander powder gives the chicken a special flavour. Ensure the chicken pieces are fried on low-medium heat

Chicken ~ 1 medium size
Coriander powder ~ 4 heaped tbsp
Onions ~ 3, sliced
Garlic ~ 1, sliced
Ginger ~ 1 inch, sliced
Turmeric powder ~ ½ tsp
Oil ~ ¾ cup
Curry leaves ~ 6
Water ~ ½ cup
Salt ~ to taste

Grind the coriander powder to a paste. Mix all the ingredients, add water and cook till the meat is done and all the water is dried up.

When the oil rises on top, fry the meat and the masala (spices) in the oil for about ten minutes and the masala coats the meat well.

molagu erachi curry

CAPSICUM AND GREEN CHILLI CHICKEN

Paradesi Jews, Queenie Hallegua

The addition of capsicum changes the flavour of the curry.This recipe is most likely to have emerged much later since capsicum was not a commonly used local ingredient

Chicken ~ 1
Onions sliced ~ 3 large
Capsicum deseeded and cubed ~ 2
Green chillies slit ~ 5 to 6
Chilli powder ~ 1 tbsp
Ginger garlic paste ~ 2 tsp
Turmeric ~ ½ tsp
Tomatoes cubed ~ 2 large
Tamarind juice [extracted from one ball, an inch in diameter and ½ cup water]
Salt ~ to taste
Sugar ~ ½ tsp
Curry leaves ~ A small sprig
Oil ~ ½ cup
Water ~ ½ cup

Heat oil in a deep vessel and fry the onion, green chillies, curry leaves till light brown. Add the turmeric powder and then the tomatoes and continue sautéing for a minute. Add ginger garlic paste and chilli powder and fry well till the oil separates.

Add the chicken and salt and mix well till the masala coats the meat. Add water to cover the chicken and cook.

When half-done add the capsicum and the sugar and continue cooking over slow flame until the oil floats on top.

Paradesi Jews from an old family album

Koubbah is a must during the Festival of Lights. Although it involves time in its preparation, koubbah speaks of the traditional celebration of the Cochinni Jews with a local flavour. Coriander leaves are also replaced with mint or celery

koubbah

Paradesi Jews, Queenie Hallegua

for the filling

1. Breast of one chicken
   Water ~ 1 cup
   Turmeric ~ ¼ tsp
   Salt ~ to taste
2. Onions ~ 3, diced
   Green chillies ~ 5
   Garlic ~ 8 cloves
   Turmeric powder ~ ¼ tsp
   Curry leaves ~ 5
   Coriander leaves ~ 1 bunch
   Oil ~ 2 tbsp
   Flour/Maida ~ 1 cup
3. Stock from the breast of chicken
   Onion ~ 1
   Coriander powder ~ 1 tbsp
   Turmeric powder ~ 1 tsp
   Green chillies ~ 3
   Curry leaves ~ 5
   Tomatoes ~ 2, diced
   Oil ~ ¼ cup
   Vinegar and salt ~ to taste

making the filling for koubbah

Boil the chicken with the rest of the ingredients in set 1. Keep aside.

Mince the onions, squeeze out all its water and keep aside. Mince the cooked chicken, green chillies and coriander leaves together.

Add the minced onions to the chicken mixture along with the turmeric powder and salt.

Make marble sized balls from the dough and flatten them.

Place some filling in its centre and seal the edges to form a 'koubbah'. Place all the koubbah balls on a greased plate and keep aside.

making the gravy

Heat the oil in a pan and sauté the curry leaves and green chillies.

Add the turmeric powder, coriander powder and fry well.

Add tomatoes and continue cooking for a minute. Add the stock and the salt when the liquid comes to a boil.

Add the koubbah one by one into the gravy and add the vinegar and salt. Let it simmer over low heat till cooked.

kozhi ishtew

CHICKEN STEW

Syrian Christian, Mary Mathew Madathikunnel

The stew changes in flavour from community to community.The base of the stew comes from the brown stew recipe

Chicken ~ 1.5-2 kg, cut small
Potatoes ~ 2, cubed large
Coconut ~ 3-4 cups, shredded
Cinnamon ~ 2, 1" sticks
Cloves ~ 8
Cardamom ~ 6, whole
Pepper ~ 2 tsp, whole
Green chillies ~ 6, whole
Ginger ~ 2" long, finely sliced
Onions ~ 2, thinly sliced
Oil ~ 2 tbsp
All purpose flour ~ 1 tsp
Salt ~ to taste
Curry leaves ~ 6-7 leaves

for the seasoning

Ghee ~ 1 tbsp
Shallots ~ 6, sliced fine
Curry leaves ~ 4-5

Take first extract coconut milk with 1½ cups water and second milk with 3 cups of water. Crush cinnamon cloves, cardamom and pepper.

Heat oil. Crush all the spices and add to the oil to sauté. Now add the ginger, chillies, onion and continue sautéing till the onion slices are transparent in colour. Pour the second milk add salt and allow it to boil. Add the chicken pieces and cook well on medium flame. When done, mix the flour with the first milk and add to the stew.

When it starts to boil, remove from fire. Heat the ghee and fry the onion slices till golden brown, along with a few curry leaves added in the end. Add to the stew and stir gently.

Take it off the heat and serve hot.

tharavu curry

DUCK GREEN CURRY

Syrian Christian, Thresiama Eapen Kadamapuzha

Green curry comes specifically from the colour of the curry. Omission of turmeric and red chilli specifically means a different flavour

Duck ~ 1, cut into pieces
Onion ~ 1, sliced
Fennel seeds ~ 1 tbsp
Cinnamon ~ 1 piece, 2 inches
Cloves ~ 8
Garlic cloves ~ ¼ cup
Ginger ~ 1 piece, 2"
Potatoes ~ 2, boiled and cubed large. 2, julienne and fried
Coconut milk ~ ½ cup, first milk
Salt ~ to taste
Vinegar ~ as required
Water ~ as required
Oil ~ to fry

Grind all the ingredients with water to get a thick paste. Take half of the paste and mix with one tbsp of vinegar and salt in two tbsp of water.

Marinate the duck pieces with this paste and keep aside for half an hour. In a cup of water, cook the duck pieces till tender. Remove the pieces from the gravy and keep aside.

Heat oil in a shallow pan and fry the duck pieces to a light brown. Using the same oil, heat two tbsp or as required, separately and add the sliced onion. When it turns colour, add the rest of the ground spices and sauté well. When done, add the gravy, the boiled potatoes and the duck pieces and let it simmer on medium heat.

When the gravy begins to thicken, add the coconut milk and switch the flame off. Garnish with fried potatoes.

kozhi chathachita roast

CHICKEN ROAST WITH CRUSHED SPICES

Syrian Christian, Thresiama Eapen Kadamapuzha

Additional ingredients like tomato sauce or ketchup were added to traditional recipes much later by homemakers, as kokies began to improvise recipes to add a 'dish' flavour, as they called it. A 'dish' was often the term used for the special recipes served at a function or a party, which had a slight leaning towards the Anglican or 'foreign' way of life. An extra aura of sophistication was lent when a 'dish' was served. This trend is seen in both Syrian and Latin cuisines

Chicken ~ 1.4 kg, pieces
Onion ~ 2
Garlic ~ ¼ cup
Ginger ~ 1, 2"
Green chillies ~ 6, sliced
Perumjeerakum (shah jeera) ~ 1 tbsp
Cinnamon ~ 2"
Cloves ~ 6
Cardamoms ~ 6
Cardamoms ~ 6-8, crushed
Turmeric powder ~ 1 tsp
Tomato ~ 4
Potatoes ~ 2 large, peeled and cubed
Tomato sauce ~ 2 tbsp
Salt ~ to taste
Oil ~ for frying

Grind all ingredients together. Place the chicken pieces in a shallow vessel, add all the crushed ingredients and one onion to it. Add enough water to cover the chicken pieces and place the peeled potatoes on top of it.

Cover the vessel and let it cook on medium heat. When the meat is tender, remove from the gravy and keep aside. Heat sufficient oil in a shallow frying pan and roast the chicken to a golden brown.

Using the same oil in another pan, fry the sliced onions and potato pieces and keep aside. Take two tablespoons of the oil and add the gravy and tomato sauce to it.

Add the fried chicken, onions and potatoes to it. Let it simmer on low to medium heat till thick.

The chicken roast can be baked in an oven before serving.

kazhal kothiyathu

MINCED LIVER FRY

Latin Catholic, Annie Burleigh

When choppers were not available, quick and constant chopping of the meat on a large wooden board (with two knives on either hand) was how the liver was minced to a fine form. A task that required not only strength but also precision. Surprisingly, liver minced this way provides a more wholesome flavour than using a mincer

Beef liver ~ ½ kg
Shallots ~ A fistful
Black pepper ~ ½ tsp, crushed
Oil

In a chopper mince together the liver chunks and shallots, till fine. In a shallow pan, heat oil. Add the chopped meat and fry, stirring constantly.

Serve hot with fresh bread.

devilled beef

Latin Catholic, Annie Burleigh

A very anglicised recipe, this is found only in specific regions of western influence in Kerala. My grandmother served this curry with puttu for Sunday breakfast after morning mass

Beef ~ 1 kilo, cut into pieces
Coriander powder ~ 1½ tbsp
Chilli powder ~ 1 tsp
Cumin (jeera) ~ 1¼ tsp
Cinnamon ~ 4 pieces of an inch length
Cloves ~ 6
Crushed pepper ~ 1 tsp
Green chillies ~ 5
Oil ~ ¼ cup
Potatoes ~ 4, quartered
Carrots ~ 3, one inch pieces
Onions ~ 5, quartered
Shallots ~ 10, sliced fine
Sugar ~ 1½ tbsp
Vinegar ~ to taste
Salt ~ to taste
Oil ~ ¼ cup
Flour ~ 1 tbsp
Water ~ 3 cups

Grind the cumin, coriander and chilli powder and mix the spices with the beef pieces and water.

Add green chillies, cloves, cinnamon, pepper, vinegar and salt to the meat and place the dish on the fire. When half done, add the carrots, potatoes and onions.

When cooked, remove the beef pieces and fry in oil till light brown.

Sauté shallots in a pan using two tablespoons of the same oil and add to the gravy. Thicken it using flour.

Add meat to the gravy and simmer for a few minutes before taking it off the stove.

attarachi varutharachathu

MUTTON FRY

Syrian Christian, Parayil family

A delicious recipe, it is a heavy preparation in terms of the meat and spices used. Frying the spice mixture changes the consistency and flavour of the spices

Mutton ~ 1 kg, pieces
Bengal gram ~ 200 gm
Onions ~ 2 large, sliced
Green chillies ~ 8, chopped
Turmeric ~ 2 tsp
Cloves ~ 6
Cinnamon ~ 4 pieces
Water ~ 2 cups
Salt ~ to taste

for the gravy

Coconut ~ 2 cups, scraped
Garlic ~ 10
Shallots ~ 10
Tomatoes ~ 4, sliced
Turmeric ~ ½ tsp
Chilli powder ~ ½ tsp
Coriander powder ~ 2 tsp
Oil ~ 1 tbsp

Cook the meat in the ingredients and keeping aside some of the sliced onion for later use.

Fry the coconut, garlic and shallots in a heavy bottomed pan in oil. When it starts to brown, add the coriander powder. Immediately remove the pan from the fire and add the remaining powders.

Grind it while still hot and add the ground paste to the meat.

Add sliced tomatoes and simmer for five minutes.

Fry the remaining onions and curry leaves, use as garnish.

pepper water

Latin Catholic, Annie Burleigh

A spicy meat soup, pepper water is also found in other parts of India with small variations in ingredients. The vegetarian version of pepper water is popular in Tamil Nadu and drunk as a soup–milagu-tannir, adopted by the Anglo-Indian community and renamed mulligatawny

for the mutton stock

Freshly crushed pepper ~ ½ tsp
Mutton bones with shreds of meat ~ ½ kg
Shallots ~ 20
Oil or ghee
Shallots ~ 3 litres

Sauté shallots in oil or ghee. Season with pepper. Cook till shallots turn light brown. Add to the stock and serve hot.

to prepare the stock

Cook ½ kg stock bones in three litres of water and 6-8 shallots sliced. Sieve to obtain stock. Remove excess fat.

kozhi roast

PEPPER CHICKEN ROAST

Latin Catholic, Annie Burleigh

This quick and easy recipe found a delicious chicken roast to serve to sudden guests at my grandmother's table. Even today, it is the most popular form in which chicken is prepared in the family

Whole chicken ~ 1½ kg [remove gizzard, heart and liver and keep aside]
Freshly crushed pepper ~ ½ tbsp
Onions ~ 3 medium sized, sliced
Corn starch ~ 1½ tsp
Salt ~ to taste
Oil for frying ~ 2 tbsp
Water ~ 2½ cups

In a deep pan, cook the chicken and the removed parts with the sliced onions, pepper and salt. Once done, remove from the gravy.

Heat oil in a wok and over medium heat, fry the chicken till brown.

Thicken the gravy using flour. Pour the gravy over the chicken and serve with fried potatoes and carrots.

tharavu curry

SPICY DUCK CURRY

Anglo-Indian, Hilda Rodrigues

This recipe does well with a dash of coconut milk. An option is to serve the curry semi-dry as the gravy coats the duck

Duck ~ 1 large, sliced into pieces
Ginger ~ 1, 3" piece, sliced
Garlic ~ 15 cloves, sliced
Green chillies ~ 4, sliced
Chilli powder ~ 3 tsp
Turmeric powder ~ 1 tsp
Pepper powder ~ 2½ tbsp
Cloves ~ 7
Cardamom ~ 8
Cinnamon ~ 2 sticks
Oil ~ ¼ cup
Juice of two limes
Salt ~ to taste

Clean the duck and marinate it with the juice of one lemon and salt.

Keep aside. Roast and rind the cloves, cardamom and cinnamon to make the spice powder.

In a vessel, heat the oil and sauté onions till it changes colour. Add the garlic, ginger and green chillies and continue sautéing.

Add the chilli powder, turmeric powder and pepper powder. Once done, add the freshly ground spice till it cooks.

Add the duck and pour enough water to cover the pieces. Cook till the meat is tender.

Taste to add salt and lime if required. Let the gravy thicken.

beef ball curry

Anglo-Indian, Howard La'frenais

This curry is light in spices and perfect with rice or freshly baked bread

for the balls

Beef ~ 1 kg, minced
Shallots ~ 15
Large onion ~ 1
Green chillies ~ 5
Ginger ~ 2" long
Pepper powder ~ 2 tbsp
Spice powder of cinnamon and cloves ~ 1 tsp
Salt ~ to taste
Eggs ~ 2, separated

for the gravy

Coriander powder ~ 3 tbsp
Chilli powder ~ 1 tbsp
Pepper powder ~ 1 tbsp
Spice powder- 1 tsp
Saffron ~ 1 tsp
Onion sliced ~ 1
Green chillies, slit into two ~ 2
Curry leaves ~ 5
Coconut ~ 1, first and second milk
Vinegar ~ 1 tbsp
Oil ~ 2½ tbsp
Salt ~ to taste

Coarsely grind shallots and onion together and mix into the mincemeat.

Finely chop the green chillies and ginger, and add them along with the pepper powder, spice powder, salt and egg yolks. Mix well.

Make small balls from the meat mixture (the size of a lime) and keep aside.

Grind the coriander powder, chilli powder, pepper powder, spice powder and saffron together and keep the spice aside.

In a pan, heat oil and sauté the onion slices if they turn translucent.

Add the green chillies, curry leaves, the ground spices and cook well. When done, add water and one cup of the second milk along with the vinegar. Allow the gravy to bubble.

Dip each meatball into the egg white and drop them one by one into the gravy. When cooked, add the first milk of the coconut. Allow the gravy to simmer before turning the gas off.

pork vindhaloo

Anglo-Indian, Howard La'frenais

Pork vindhaloo prepared in Anglo Indian and Latin homes in Kerala is different from those found in other parts of India like Goa. The number of spices is fewer. A must at every occasion in my parental home, it can be eaten with any staple. Using coconut vinegar gives a very unique flavour

1. Pork ~ 1 kg
   Large onion ~ 1, ground
   Shallots ~ 15
   Ripe tomatoes ~ 2, blanched and pureed
   Oil ~ ½ cup
   Curry leaves ~ 5
   Water ~ 1½ cups
   Vinegar ~ 2 tbsp
   Salt ~ to taste
   Sugar ~ 1 tsp
2. Chilli powder ~ 5 tbsp
   Turmeric powder ~ 1 tsp
   Small cumin ~ 1 tsp
   Mustard seeds ~ 2 tbsp
   Garlic cloves ~ 8
   Ginger ~ 1, 2" piece
   Vinegar ~ 2 tbsp

Grind together the ingredients under set 2.

In a pressure cooker, fry the ground masala. Once cooked and the oil rises above, add the ground onion and sauté till brown. Add the tomato puree and the curry leaves with the salt and two tablespoons of vinegar.

Add the pork along with the sugar. Place the lid of the cooker and pressure cook with the weight for ten minutes.

Once cooked, allow the gravy to thicken.

tharavu roast

SLICED DUCK ROAST

Syrian Christian, Parayil family

The recipe is not heavy in terms of spices, the meat is allowed to carry its own flavour

Duck ~ 1, cut into large pieces with skin
Onions ~ 4 large, sliced
Green chillies ~ 8, chopped
Ginger
Garlic ~ 2 pods, peeled and diced
Cardamom ~ 5
Cloves ~ 5
Cinnamon ~ 2 medium pieces, powdered
Pepper ~ 2 tbsp
Turmeric ~ 2 tbsp
Curry leaves ~ 3 sprigs
Potato ~ 1 large, sliced
Oil ~ ½ cup
Vinegar and salt ~ to taste

Cook the duck with 1 tablespoon of the pepper and 1 tablespoon of the turmeric powder and the remaining ingredients. Remove the pieces from the gravy and fry in hot oil and keep aside. To the gravy, add the remaining pepper and turmeric. Pour the gravy into the oil used for frying the duck and let it thicken. Once it thickens, add the fried duck and let the gravy coat the pieces.

Garnish with fried potatoes.

muzhuvan tharavu roast

WHOLE DUCK ROAST

Syrian Christian, Parayil family

A full duck is cooked on a special occasion

Duck ~ 1 kg
Onions ~ 2
Green chillies ~ 5
Ginger ~ 1 inch
Garlic ~ 4-5 cloves
Curry leaves ~ 5-6 leaves

to grind

Oil ~ 4 tbsp
Coriander ~ 2 tsp
Turmeric ~ ¼ tsp
Pepper ~ 1 tsp
Cloves ~ 6
Cinnamon ~ 1 medium piece
Cardamom ~ 3
Black cumin seeds (Shah jeera) ~ 2 tsp

Grind the ingredients and keep aside. Clean the duck and remove its neck. Add one-teaspoon vinegar and salt (to taste) to the ground paste and smear inside and outside the duck. Cook the duck in the rest of the ingredients with sufficient water to cover it. Cook till duck is done and gravy is thick. Remove the duck and fry in the oil.

Serve the fried duck with its gravy poured over it.

duck raichath

Anglo-Indian, Howard La'frenais

The use of sugar changes the flavour to a more subdued one when compared to the preparations of duck by other communities. Absence of red chilli powder and the use of coriander powder highlight a very distinct flavour

Duck, cut into pieces – 1
Onion large – 1
Ginger chopped fine – 1 tbsp
Green chillies chopped fine – 1 tbsp
Garlic chopped fine – 1 tbsp
Sugar – ½ tbsp
Coconut – 1, first and second milk
Water – ¼ cup
Oil – ¼ cup
Coriander powder – 1 tbsp
Vinegar – 2 tbsp
Salt – to taste

Cook the duck in the second milk and water. Once done, fry the pieces in a shallow dish and keep aside.

In the same oil, fry chopped ingredients. Add the coriander powder and continue frying till done. Add the duck pieces, salt, sugar, vinegar and let it simmer.

Add the first milk and continue allowing the gravy to simmer for half a minute longer. Serve hot.

anglo-indian stuffed fish in banana leaf

Anglo-Indian, Faylene Lobo

An Anglo-Indian version of the meen pollichathu (term for 'grilled in banana leaf'), valam puli can be substituted with lime-juice for a variation. This preparation also proves to be a good barbeque option. Faylene recalls how her grandmother made this dish using hot coal and a homemade grill

Fish (pomfret or mackerel) ~ 2
Shallots, sliced fine ~ 10
Green chillies ~ 3
Garlic cloves ~ 2, sliced fine
Ginger ~ ¼ inch long, sliced fine
Red dry chilli ~ 1, soaked well and deseeded
Salt ~ to taste
Kodumpulli ~ 1, soaked in water

Make a spice paste with all the ingredients and rub and stuff the fish with it. Oil a banana leaf and wrap the fish in it. Place on a pan over low heat and cover with a lid to grill, turning the fish regularly until cooked.

chilli meat

Anglo-Indian, Mertel Gomez

Prawns may be used instead of beef, which needs less cooking time. The combination of red chilli powder and pepper changes the flavour when combined with spices such as cinnamon and cloves

Beef ~ 1 kg, sliced
Chilli powder ~ 1 tbsp
Turmeric powder ~ ½ tsp
Cumin seeds ~ ½ tsp
Garlic cloves ~ 5
Cinnamon ~ 1 piece, 1½" long
Cloves ~ 2
Pepper powder ~ ¼ tsp
Potatoes ~ 2, cubed large
Onions ~ 2, sliced fine
Water ~ 1 cup
Oil ~ for frying

Grind all the spices and mix into water. Add meat slices and boil till fairly done. Reduce the gravy to a thick consistency.

Add potato slices and cook till done.

Heat oil in a vessel and fry sliced onions. Keep aside.

Take out the meat and potatoes from the gravy and fry in the remaining hot oil. Return pieces to the gravy and simmer. Serve hot.

beef curry stew

Anglo-Indian, Mertel Gomez

A unique version of the stew, this recipe has meatballs and saffron

Beef mincemeat ~ ½ kg
Egg ~ 1
White vinegar ~ ½ tsp
Pepper powder ~ ¼ tsp
Clove powder ~ ¼ tsp
Cinnamon powder ~ ¼ tsp
Onion ~ 2, 1 sliced and the other cubed
Potatoes ~ 2, medium size
Ginger ~ ½ tsp, chopped fine
Green chillies ~ 2, chopped
Curry leaves ~ 4
White bread ~ ½ slice, soaked in water and then squeezed
Coconut ~ ½, first and second milk
Saffron ~ a pinch, to colour the milk
Salt ~ to taste

Mix minced meat with egg yolk, pepper, clove and cinnamon powder, green chillies, onion and salt. Make small balls of the meat and keep aside.

Colour the milk with saffron and keep aside.

Heat some oil and fry the onion slices to a light brown. Add ginger, curry leaves and green chillies. Add milk, onions, potatoes and salt.

When half cooked, add the meat balls dipped in a mixture of beaten egg and vinegar. Cook till done. Add first milk and once it simmers, take the pan off the heat.

beef sausage rolls

Anglo-Indian, Mertel Gomez

Homemade sausages were popular during Portuguese reign in Kerala. This one is made of beef and flavoured with local spices

Beef mince ~ 1 kg
A slice of bread, soaked in some water
Cloves ~ 12
Cinnamon stick 2" long
Salt ~ 1 tbsp spoon
Saltpetre ~ ¼ tsp
Peppercorn ~ 1 tsp
Oil ~ for frying sausages

Add salt and saltpetre to the minced meat and keep it aside. Powder all the spices and mix it into the meat.

Squeeze out the water from the bread and mix it into the meat. Make them into rolls the size of cocktail sausages and boil in half a cup of water until all the water dries up.

Fry in hot oil till brown. Serve hot.

beef chops

Anglo-Indian, Faylene Lobo

Chops were always a speciality in Anglo-Indian homes. This recipe uses curry leaves and spices, giving it a local flavour

Beef ~ 1 kg, sliced thin
Water ~ 1 cup
Peppercorns ~ 2 tbsp
Cinnamon ~ ½ tbsp
Clove ~ ½ tbsp
Chilli powder ~ ½ tbsp
Turmeric powder ~ ¼ tsp
Salt ~ to taste
Onions sliced thick ~ ¼ kg
Green chillies slit ~ 6
Ginger sliced fine ~ 1 inch
Curry leaves ~ 2 sprigs
Potatoes ~ 5, boiled and sliced round
Oil for frying ~ ½ cup

Pound the beef with a pounder and keep aside.

Cook the meat along with the spices, powders and salt in water. Once done, remove the pieces from gravy and fry them in hot oil.

Sauté the onions in the remaining oil till they turn translucent. Now, add the chillies, ginger and curry leaves and continue sautéing.

Add the cooked potatoes and meat along with the gravy. Allow the gravy to coat the meat well.

pork roast

Anglo-Indian, Faylene Lobo

This pork dish is made by Anglo-Indians as a short eat to accompany a glass of whisky or vodka. Served as it is or with mousard, a homemade mustard sauce

Pork ~ 1 kg chunk
Cabbage ~ 1
Pepper powder ~ 1 tbsp
Cinnamon ~ 2, 1" long sticks
Cloves ~ 5
Dry red chillies ~ 5
Green chillies ~ 2
Onions sliced ~ 2
Ginger sliced thin ~ ¾" long
Sugar ~ 1 tsp
Oil ~ ¼ cup
Water ~ 1 cup
Salt ~ to taste

Powder the spices and keep it aside. Heat oil in a deep pan and caramelise the sugar to a golden brown. Add the powdered spices, red chillies and the pork chunk to the oil and fry well, turning the pork regularly for a duration of five minutes. Now, add the water and the salt to it. Once the water begins to boil, cut the cabbage into four and place them on the pork, covering the pork with it. Close the pan with a lid, occasionally turning the pork till cooked.

Remove the meat from the pan and once cool, slice some fat off the cooked pork and heat it in a new pan to sauté the green chillies, onions, and ginger slices.

Add these to the gravy and allow it to thicken.

Serve sliced pork with the gravy and the steamed cabbage.

stuffed chicken

Anglo-Indian, Faylene Lobo

A special chicken roast made for Christmas, it is served dry or with gravy. To make the gravy, the Lobos spice it up by adding sautéed sliced onions, more spices (masala) and diced tomatoes which were fried in oil

Whole chicken, with skin ~ 2 kg
Peppercorns ~ 1 tbsp
Cinnamon ~ 1 stick, 1" long
Cloves ~ 5
Ginger-garlic paste ~ 1 tsp
Potatoes ~ 2, cooked
White bread cut into cubes ~ 5 slices
Dry white raisins (kishmish) ~ 20
Cashews ~ 10
Oil ~ for frying
Water ~ as required

Powder the spices and grind along with the ginger-garlic paste to form the 'masala' (spice paste).

In a pan heat some of the oil and fry the potatoes and the bread separately. Keep aside. Now fry the raisins and the cashews till light brown.

Cook the gizzard, liver and heart along with the masala and in enough water to cover them. Once done, remove and cool. Chop fine and mix with the remaining fried ingredients to form the stuffing for the chicken.

Rub the chicken with the remaining 'masala', ½ tablespoon oil and salt to taste, allowing it to seep into the skin and cavity. Stuff the chicken with the prepared stuffing and place in a baking tray. Roast in a preheated oven at 180c for 45 minutes or till cooked.

Serve fresh out of the oven, with the fried potatoes and the bread cubes on the side.

temparad

Anglo-Indian, Faylene Lobo

Raw bananas and beef make an interesting combination. A recipe found in Fort Kochi homes

Beef, cut into 1" cubes ~ 1 kg
Coriander powder ~ 2 tbsp
Chilli powder ~ ½ tbsp
Pepper powder ~ ¼ tsp
Cinnamon ~ ¼ tsp powdered
Clove powder ~ ¼ tsp
Turmeric powder ~ a pinch
Ginger-garlic paste ~ ¼ tsp
Cumin ~ ¼ tsp
Onions ~ 2
Curry leaves ~ 2 sprigs
Green chillies ~ 4
Garlic cloves, sliced ~ 4
Ginger, sliced ~ 1, ¼" long
Toddy vinegar ~ 1 tbsp (toddy vinegar can be substituted with white vinegar)
Raw Kerala plantain or potatoes ~ 2, sliced round
Coconut ~ 1, first milk
Water ~ ¾ cup
Salt ~ to taste
Oil ~ for cooking

Make a thick masala of the spices by grinding them together with sufficient water and keep aside. In a pan, heat the oil and sauté the curry leaves, onions, chillies, garlic and ginger.

Add the meat to this along with salt and enough water to cook it. When half cooked, add the raw bananas and continue cooking. When almost done, and the coconut milk is and allow the dish to simmer for a few minutes. Serve hot.

attarachi alisa

ALISA WITH LAMB

Malabar Mappila, Rafiza

Alisa is a heavy dish of the Mappila Muslims of the Malabar. Using sugar with it is a tradition practised by the community

Wheat ~ 2 cups, broken
Fat of lamb/erachi kozhupu ~ 50 gm
Cinnamon ~ 1 piece, 2" long
Onion ~ 1 small, chopped
Ghee ~ 30 gm
Salt ~ to taste

Cook all of the above ingredients in a thick bottomed vessel.

When done, use a firm wooden rod and beat till it becomes a thick consistency (The mixture can be blended in a blender/ food processor as well, making a thick paste or gravy).

Make a small dip in the centre of the mixture and pour the ghee into it, allowing it to seep in.

Serve with sugar on the side.

attarachi biryani

MALABAR MUTTON BIRYANI

Malabar Mappila, Rafiza

Very well known for this special biryani, the community takes great pride in its unique flavours and preparation. Flavours change slightly from home to home, but the central ingredients remain the same. Interestingly, jeera rice is used instead of basmati. This dish is considered having originated from the community's Middle Eastern ancestry

For the rice

Jeera samba rice ~ 1 kg
Mutton pieces ~ 1 kg
Onion ~ 1 kg, julienne (¾ cup for masala and ¼ cup for rice)
Green chillies ~ 200 gm
Ginger-garlic paste from 50 gm of each
Garam masala ~ 1 tbsp
Lime ~ 1
Tomato ~ 3
Water ~ 9 cups
Coriander ~ 1 bunch
Mint ~ 1 bunch
Ghee ~ 50 gm
Sunflower oil ~ 150 gm
Cashew nuts ~ 50 gm
Raisins ~ 20 gm
Curd ~ ¾ cup

preparing the spices and meat

Clean the mutton and keep aside.

In a deep pan, add 2 tbsp oil and 1 tbsp ghee. Add onions and sauté [to hasten the process, later add a pinch of salt].

In a deep pan add oil and one tbsp of ghee. Add onions and sauté till it changes colour.

Add ginger garlic, tomatoes and the meat to cook. When almost done, add the curd and cook till the meat is done.

Clean the rice and keep it aside. In a pan, add remaining ghee and oil. Add the onions and brown them.

Add the cashew nuts and when golden brown, add the raisins. Remove and keep aside once the raisins swell.

Add the rice to the pan and fry till it turns crisp.

Bring water to a boil and add to the rice. Add salt to taste and cook till done. Layer the rice with the cooked meat and sprinkle mint leaves and ghee on top. Heat a girdle on medium flame and place the biryani pot on it (cover with a lid) and bake in an oven for 15 minutes or till the gravy of the meat evaporates. Serve hot.

malabar ishtew

MUTTON STEW

Malabar Mappila, Rasheeda and Rahima Meethalakath

The Malabari ishtew is very popular in all local Malabar households, and is also made with chicken or vegetables. Spices are added according to the potency required; some families prepare the ishtew with 10-12 fresh green chillies

Mutton ~ 1 kg with bone, medium pieces
Onion ~ 4, sliced
Tomatoes ~ 3
Green chillies ~ 4, slit
Ginger ~ 1 tsp, paste
Garlic ~ 1 tsp, paste
Cloves ~ 2 pieces
Cinnamon ~ 1 piece, 2" long
Pepper ~ 1½ tbsp, crushed
Star anise ~ 1, broken into pieces
Coriander leaves/curry leaves ~ 1 small bunch/1 sprig
Coconut milk ~ first and second milk, 2 cups each
Oil ~ 2 tbsp
Salt ~ to taste

for the garnish

Oil ~ 1 tbsp
Shallots ~ 4-5
Coriander/curry leaves ~ A few

Sauté the spices, green chillies and the onions in the oil. When the onions turn colour, add the curry leaves or coriander leaves.

Now, add the second milk, crushed peppercorns and salt along with the meat and potatoes.

After the meat is cooked, let the gravy simmer. Then add the first milk and let it boil once and switch off the flame.

For the garnish, heat the oil and sauté the shallots and the curry leaves. If using coriander, it should be added fresh.

Add the garnish to the ishtew and serve hot.

haleem

SOUPY MUTTON STEW

Malabar Mappila, Rasheeda and Rahima Meethalakath

A soupy dish, it is made during Ramadan or Ramzaan. The version differs from the one found in the North of India, which was brought by Persian invaders. The recipe which came from the Middle East to Kerala adopted local preparation methods and spices

Chicken ~ 1 kg
Broken wheat ~ 1 kg
Onions ~ 4 large, sliced
Tomatoes ~ 3, diced
Green chillies ~ 10, sliced
Ginger and garlic paste ~ 2 tsp
Red chilli powder ~ 2 tsp
Coriander powder ~ 1 tsp
Turmeric powder ~ 1 tsp
Salt ~ to taste
Cashewnuts ~ 10
Coriander leaves ~ 1 small bunch

Cook the wheat well and keep aside. Marinate the chicken in the remaining ingredients (except for the ¼ cup sliced onions) for about half an hour and cook in sufficient water.

Heat the oil and shallow fry the chicken. Remove the flesh from the pieces and keep aside.

Add the gravy to the oil used to fry the chicken and thicken.

Now, add the cooked wheat and coconut milk.

Fry the remaining onions and the cashewnuts golden brown and garnish the dish along with the coriander leaves.

petti pathari

FRIED BOX BREAD WITH CHICKEN AND EGG FILLING

Malabar Mappila, Rasheeda and Rahima Meethalakath

'Petti' refers to 'box' in Malayalam and this dish can be prepared with any meat of one's preference. The casing is also rolled out to form a thin bread, eaten on its own with curries or sweetened coconut milk by adding sugar. This is a staple for Iftar in Mappila homes

for the filling

Chicken ~ ¼ kg
Large onions ~ 3, finely minced
Green chillies ~ 5, chopped fine
Garlic ~ 4 flakes
Garlic ~ ½ tsp, paste
Ginger paste ~ ½ tsp, paste
Turmeric powder ~ ¼ tsp
Chilli powder ~ 2 tsp
Garam masala powder ~ ¼ tsp
Coriander leaves ~ a small bunch
Salt ~ to taste
Oil ~ 1-2 tbsp
Oil ~ for frying

Cook the chicken with the garlic flakes, turmeric and chilli powders and salt. Debone the chicken and shred the meat. In a pan, sauté the green chillies, garlic, ginger in oil. Add the onions and once it changes colour, add the shredded meat, the garam masala and the coriander leaves. Cook till the chicken is coated well.

for the casing

All-purpose flour/maida ~ 2 cups
Oil ~ 1 tbsp
Water ~ as required
Salt ~ 1¼ tsp
Boiled eggs ~ 2 (half the number of patharies made)

Mix all the casing ingredients together, adding water slowly to obtain a soft dough consistency.

For the casing make a thin square, add some of the prepared filling and place half of a boiled egg in it, with the yolk facing downward.

Seal the casing firmly with another square by pasting the sides together. Heat oil in a deep pan and drop the petti pathari one by one, removing them as they turn a golden brown.

pidi

CHICKEN STEW WITH SEMOLINA BALLS

Malabari Jews, Ilanit Menachem

Semolina is used more in Jewish cooking than any other cuisine. This version of the stew is unseen elsewhere in Kerala

Chicken ~ 1 kg, deboned and cubed
Onions ~ 2, diced
Garlic ~ 3 cloves
Coconut ~ ½ cup, shredded
Black pepper and salt ~ to taste
Semolina ~ ¾ cup
Water ~ 1 cup, boiling
Coconut ~ ½ cup, shredded
Salt ~ to taste
All-purpose flour ~ ½ cup

Heat the oil and fry a slice of onion, add the chicken and fry till browned. Add the water and let it simmer on low heat.

Prepare the semolina balls by adding the semolina, salt, coconut to boiling water and mix well.

Add the flour gradually to make dough. Knead the dough and with your palms make balls the size of a gooseberry and add to the chicken.

Grind the coconut with the garlic and water and add this to the pot.

Add the pepper and salt and let it simmer on medium flame for half an hour till all flavours are infused. Serve hot.

kalafom

PIE WITH HERBS

Malabari Jews, Ilanit Menachem

The addition of curry leaves and green chillies makes the recipe unique to Kerala Jews

Onions ~ 2, sliced fine
Curry leaves ~ 2 sprigs, finely chopped
Coriander leaves ~ ½ cup, finely chopped
Mint leaves ~ ½ cup, finely chopped
Green chilli ~ 1, finely chopped
Zucchini ~ 1, finely grated
Oil ~ ½ cup
Baking powder ~ 1 tsp
Sugar ~ 2 tbsp
Vinegar ~ 1 tbsp
Semolina ~ 1½ cups
Coconut ~ ¾ cups, shredded
Eggs ~ 2
Water ~ 1 cup
Salt ~ 1 tsp

Mix all ingredients well. The batter can be then baked in an oven at 175 degrees till done or pan baked by lightly greasing a pan with oil and pouring the mixture in scoops at a time and allowing it to rise, to make pancake sized kalafom.

puzcku

SWEET YELLOW CHICKEN CURRY

Malabari Jews, Ilanit Menachem

Ilanit Menachem says honey is an addition to the original recipe and a favourite with children

Chicken ~ 1 whole, skinned and pieced
Potatoes ~ 4, diced
Onions ~ 2, sliced
Garlic cloves ~ 5, sliced
Salt ~ to taste
Black pepper ~ ½ tsp
Turmeric ~ ½ tsp
Dry ginger powder ~ ½ tsp
Honey ~ 2 tbsp
Vinegar ~ 1 tbsp
Oil ~ 6 tbsp

Fry the onion, when it begins to brown, add the garlic.

Add the chicken pieces and the water till cooked.

Alongside, fry the potato cubes until browned on all sides.

Add the salt, pepper, turmeric and vinegar to the chicken. Add a little more water if more sauce is required.

Next, add the honey and mix well. Add the diced fried potatoes and simmer for about 40 minutes. Stir occasionally till the gravy is thick and coats the chicken well. Serve hot.

folitz'zh

CHICKEN IN HERBS

Malabari Jews, Ilanit Menachem

Eaten on Saturdays as a special dish, this dish gathers more flavour when kept overnight and warmed in an oven

Chicken ~ 1 medium size, small pieces
Black pepper ~ 1 tsp
Coriander powder ~ 1 tsp
Ginger paste ~ 1 tsp
Salt ~ to taste
Oil ~ 2 tbsp

for the gravy

Fresh coriander leaves ~ ½ bunch, chopped
Celery ~ 4 stalks, chopped
Mint ~ ½ cup, chopped
Garlic ~ 5 cloves
Onions ~ 2, diced
Tomato paste ~ 2 tsp
Chilli powder ~ 1 tsp
Black pepper ~ 1 tsp
Ginger ~ 1 tsp
Coriander powder ~ 1 tsp
Vinegar ~ 1 tbsp
Salt ~ to taste

Garnish

Potatoes ~ 1 large, sliced and fried to a golden brown

Marinate the chicken in a paste of the ingredients and leave in the refrigerator for three hours.

Heat the oil in a deep pan and fry the chicken pieces. Keep aside. Grind the coriander leaves, mint, celery and 2 garlic cloves, and 1 onion.

Heat some oil in a pan and fry the remaining garlic and onion. When it turns colour, add the paste and sauté well. Add the tomato paste, spices and vinegar.

Cook for a few minutes and add the chicken pieces. Let the dish lightly simmer on low to medium heat for about 30 minutes.

Decorate with fried potatoes and serve hot.

aisfti

SPICY BEEF STEW

Malabari Jews, Ilanit Menachem

This stew has a distinct flavour because of the blend of spices that come from Jewish religious customs. It is slightly heavier in flavour than the Ishtew and other stew variations found in Kerala

Beef ~ 1.5 kg, cubed
Garlic ~ 3-4 cloves, sliced
Vinegar ~ 2 tbsp
Tomatoes ~ 6, diced
Tamarind ~ 1 tbsp
Tomato paste ~ 1 tbsp
Chilli powder ~ 1 tsp
Black pepper ~ ½ tsp
Ginger ~ 1 piece, sliced
Coriander powder ~ 1 tsp
Turmeric powder ~ ½ tsp

Fry the onions and garlic in oil. Add the meat and fry. Add water to cover the beef.

Now, add the vinegar, tomatoes, pepper and salt. Cook till the meat is tender.

Add the spices and tomato paste and continue to cook with the gravy coating the beef well. Decorate with fried potatoes.

mollvou kuthan

SPICY RED CHICKEN

Malabari Jews, Ilanit Menachem

The original recipe does not contain tomato paste, which was added by the Cochinni women on reaching Israel and improvising the recipe. Potatoes can be fried beforehand, which offers an even better flavour. Chillies and red chilli powder can be increased based on the hotness required

Chicken ~ 1.5 kg, pieces
Onions ~ 2 sliced
Garlic cloves ~ 4, sliced
Green chilli ~ 1, sliced
Tomatoes ~ 5, diced
Tomato paste ~ 2 tbsp
Tamarind ~ 1 tbsp, heaped
Potatoes ~ 3, diced
Pepper powder ~ ½ tsp
Dry ginger powder ~ ½ tsp
Red chilli powder ~ ½ tsp
Turmeric ~ ½ tsp
Coriander powder ~ ½ tsp
Salt ~ to taste

Fry the onions and garlic. Add the chicken and fry till it changes colour to white. Add the green chilli and vinegar.

Now add the tomatoes, tomato paste, tamarind, and bring it to a boil on low flame. Add the potatoes, spices, and the tomato paste and let it simmer for 45 minutes.

Serve hot.

beef balls stew

Malabari Jews, Ilanit Menachem

This dish is best served with rice or Cochin couscous

for the balls

Beef ~ ½ kg, minced
Onion ~ 1, diced
Garlic cloves ~ 3, diced
Curry leaves ~ 1 small bunch, chopped
Coriander leaves ~ 1 small bunch, chopped
Mint leaves ~ 1 small bunch, chopped
Red chilli powder ~ 1 tsp
Coriander powder ~ 1 tsp
Salt ~ 1 tsp
Black pepper powder ~ ½ tsp
Turmeric powder ~ ½ tsp
Eggs ~ 2
Breadcrumbs ~ 3 tbsp

for the sauce

Onions ~ 1, chopped
Tomatoes ~ 3, chopped
Coriander ~ 1 tsp
Red chilli powder ~ 1 tsp
Salt ~ 1 tsp
Turmeric powder ~ ½ tsp
Black pepper powder ~ ½ tsp
Tomato paste ~ 4 tbsp
Tamarind ~ 1 tbsp
Water ~ 1½ cups

Mix the minced meat with all ingredients and keep in the fridge for half an hour. Make patties or balls the size of gooseberries.

For the sauce, heat oil and fry the onions. When it turns colour add the tomato puree. Let it simmer for a few minutes, and add the remaining ingredients for the sauce one by one, stirring in between.

Let the mixture boil. Add the meatballs and continue cooking till the gravy thickens.

kozhi alias

ALISA WITH CHICKEN

Malabar Mappila, Rasheeda and Rahima Meethalakath

Interestingly, the ingredients of the chicken alias is very different from the lamb, bringing forth a completely different flavour

Broken wheat ~ 1 kg
Chicken ~ 1 kg
Garlic ~ 3 pods
Onions ~ 3 large
Cashewnuts ~ 10
Ghee ~ 1 tbsp
Oil ~ ½ tbsp
Salt ~ to taste

Soak the wheat overnight and wash and drain it in the morning. Cook the wheat and chicken together, along with the onions, garlic and salt. Once well cooked (to almost a mash), remove the bones of the chicken from the pieces.

Fry the cashewnuts in ghee and add this to the mixture of meat and cooked wheat. Decorate the top with a few cashewnuts and serve hot.

pashiue erchi

JEWISH LAMB STEW

Malabari Jews, Ilanit Menachem

A light stew, very different from those of the other communities. The flavour of the lamb stock comes from the mild spices and the tangy flavour of tomatoes. The quantities of chilli powder and green chillies are adjusted according to the flavours needed. Use of coriander seeds is what gives the stew a distinct flavour

Lamb ~ 1½ kg, cubed
Onions ~ 2, sliced
Garlic cloves ~ 5, sliced
Green chilli ~ 1, sliced
Vinegar ~ 2 tbsp
Tomatoes ~ 6, diced
Tomato paste ~ 2 tbsp
Red chilli powder ~ 1 tsp
Black pepper powder ~ ½ tsp
Ginger ~ 1 piece, diced
Coriander seeds ~ ½ tsp
Turmeric powder ~ ½ tsp
Crocus ~ ½ tsp
Salt ~ to taste

Heat the oil in a pan and fry the onions and garlic till they change colour. Add the lamb and fry well, turning the pieces occasionally.

Add the pepper, vinegar and tomatoes and cook well. Now, add the spices and tomato paste. Let it simmer to medium heat till the lamb is cooked and soft. Add the potatoes just before the lamb is completely done.

pork acharu

PORK PICKLE

Syrian Christian, Parayil family

Pickle made of pork is found only in Christian homes in Kerala. Although fish and beef pickles are most commonly made, pork pickle is a delicacy relished for its distinct taste

Pork ~ 1 kg, pieces
Oil ~ 1.5 cups
Vinegar ~ ¾ cup
Chilli powder ~ ½ cup
Ginger ~ 3 pieces, sliced fine
Garlic ~ 1 pod, sliced fine
Cardamom ~ 2
Cloves ~ 2
Cinnamon ~ 2 pieces
Fenugreek ~ ½ tsp
Mustard seeds ~ 1 tsp
Salt ~ to taste

Marinate the pork pieces in one-teaspoon salt and keep aside for half an hour. Wash the meat and keep aside to drain.

Grind all the remaining ingredients in a few tablespoons of vinegar. Heat the oil and fry the meat pieces on high flame, stirring while cooking. Remove the fried pork, reduce flame and to the same oil add the ground masala (the spices) and cook till done.

Add the meat, the remaining vinegar and salt. Cook on medium heat for 7-8 minutes.

chorka

VINEGAR

Shared by a Malabari Jew; sourced from Annie Burleigh Kurishingal's notes

The Jews of Kerala prepared vinegar from raisins used for making wine

Raisins (after making wine) ~ 4 cups
Water ~ 8 cups

Mix the raisins with the water and place in a *bharani* (urn). Let it sit for 2 to 2.5 months. The vinegar will be ready in that period of time

A congregation of Jews in Kerala

It is said that Jewish women plied across to Kochi from Paravur and Chendamangalam (previous Jewish settlements before they moved to Israel) on canoes to sell their ware. The Torah talks about wine or cider being used to make vinegar. Since cider was unavailable in Kerala, Jews made vinegar with locally available raisins.

This recipe is from my paternal grandmother's recipe book, shared by a Malabari Jew friend from her 'bridal book', a book of recipes and old Jewish folk songs in Malayalam, gifted to her by her mother on her wedding day

SWEETS AND DESSERTS

ethaka appam

PLANTAIN BREAD

Latin Catholic, Annie Burleigh Kurishingal

Eaten during tea-time or as a breakfast treat, the consistency of the appam (soft to touch) depends on the careful use of rice-flour

Kerala plantains ~ 6, sliced round (very ripe)
Rice flour ~ 2 tbsp
Coconut milk ~ 1 big coconut, first milk
Sugar ~ As required

Mix the banana slices, coconut milk, flour and sugar in a vessel, ensuing the batter is not thick but of a semi-loose consistency. Pour the batter into an oiled shallow pan and steam over medium to high flame. Use a clean broomstick to check if the appam is cooked and more or less firm in consistency. When cool, it can be cut into wedges.

dutch bread

BREUDHER

Anglo-Indian, Courtesy C V Chandran, Quality Bakery, Fort Kochi

It is said that the raisins do not sink to the bottom in a breudher made well! Popular with the Anglo-Indians in Cochin, it is eaten with a generous helping of butter or with the ripe Kerala banana called chingampazham and mutton-quorma where the sweet bread is used to scoop out generous helpings of its thick gravy. Breudher is made in Fort Kochi till date at Quality Bakery, which ships large quantities of it to Anglo-Indians outside India, during Christmas. Breudher is also found in Sri Lanka, where the Dutch once ruled

Dough from flour ~ 500 gm
Eggs ~ 8, large
Butter ~ 125 gm
Sugar ~ 170 gm, caramelised
Raisins ~ 120 gm
Milk, to moisten ~ 1 tbsp
Sodium bicarbonate ~ ¼ tsp
Nutmeg ~ 2 pinches

Beat egg yolks in a large bowl. Add the butter and continue beating.

Dissolve the sodium bicarbonate in milk and keep aside.

Pour the beaten mixture into the dough followed by the caramelised sugar. Continue beating, while adding milk and half the raisins. Pour into a buttered pan and sprinkle remaining raisins on top.

Keep aside for about half an hour in a warm place for the dough to rise.

Bake in a preheated oven at 175 degree centigrade for 30 to 40 minutes.

Serve warm with butter.

khulkhuls

Anglo-Indian, Mertel Gomez

Khulkhuls are a crisp sweet snack usually made from rice flour. Reduce the sweetness by adjusting the sugar coating

Wheat/rice flour ~ 1 kg
Butter/dalda ~ 250 gm
Egg yolks ~ 12
Coconut ~ 1, first milk

Knead the flour well with the egg yolks and add a cup of thick coconut milk and butter. The dough should be supple and not too hard. Take a portion of the dough and make a medium sized ball. Hold a fork in your left hand and press this ball down evenly. Then roll up and keep aside. Repeat the process with the rest of the flour.

Heat some oil in a pan and drop a few khulkhuls at a time and fry till pale brown in colour.

For the coating, for every 500 gm of khulkhuls, take 125 gm sugar and make a thick sugar syrup.

Drop the khulkhuls into the syrup and allow it to coat them. Take the khulkhuls out and cool them. The sugar will frost the khulkhuls.

neiappam

Syrian Christian, Mary Mathew Madathikunnel

A breakfast or tea time snack, which the Jews specially prepare during Hannukah as a popular treat during the festival, neiappam is popular across Kerala and also called unniyappam. Some recipes call for the use of wheat flour in the same proportion as rice flour and some use dry ginger powder. Banana is also omitted, although the original recipe calls for the addition of banana

Rice flour ~ 1 cup
Water ~ ½ cup
Jaggery ~ 1 cup
Kerala banana ~ 1
Cardamom ~ a few, powdered
Oil or ghee for frying
Sodium bicarbonate ~ 1 tsp

Mash the banana well and mix it with the rice flour. Melt the jaggery in the water, allow it to cool. Once cool, add it to the rice mixture along with the cardamom powder and sodium bicarbonate. Make a loose batter but not runny. Pour some of the oil/ghee into (just enough to fry the appam) the *neiappamchatti* (utensil used for frying neiappam). Once hot, add the batter. Turn the neiappam using a slotted spatula, ensuring both sides are cooked and of a reddish brown colour. Serve hot.

dhol dhol

Anglo-Indian, Mertel Gomez

An Anglo-Indian snack, the rice flour gives it a soft bread-like consistency. Served with tea

Rice flour ~ 1 cup
Sugar ~ 1 cup
Cardamom ~ 1 large one (powdered)
Fresh coconuts ~ 2, use first and second milk

Mix rice flour, cardamom and sugar. Add the milk to it and keep over fire to bring to a boil. Stir constantly to obtain a thick consistency.

Pour into a greased dish and cut into square pieces when cool.

nutmeg caramel custard

Latin Catholic, Annie Burleigh

Brought by the British, caramel custard is popular in Christian homes in Kerala. Although a universal dessert, caramel custard took a twist in my grandmother's kitchen with nutmeg, coconut or a topping of caramelised fruit such as banana. My grandmother added nutmeg for an extra (tropical) flavour. She replaced a part of the milk with ¼ cup coconut milk and also made a topping of grated coconut and chopped Kerala banana mixed with caramel, which was added after unmoulding the custard. Sometimes thickened orange juice is poured over the unmoulded pudding

Milk – 1½ cups
Eggs – 2
Sugar – 2 tbsp, ¼ cup for the caramel
Vanilla essence – a few drops
Nutmeg powder – 2 pinches

Make the caramel by heating the sugar in a pan over low heat. Once golden brown, pour into the mould for the custard and set aside. In a thick-bottomed pan, boil water to make a double boiler.

Beat the eggs first and add the remaining ingredients, mixing well. Pour into the mould and place to cook by double boiling in the pan with the boiling water.

Cook for 15-20 minutes after covering the pan tight, or till done.

Once cool, remove the mould and serve the custard warm or cool.

matrimony

Anglo-Indian, Mertel Gomez

Flourless biscuits, which were always made in bulk during Christmas time, are still a favourite at the Gomez home

Cashew nuts chopped into fine bits ~ 1 cup
Sugar ~ 1½ cups
Almond flavouring (essence) or rose water

Add sugar to water to make syrup of one thread consistency. Add nuts, essence and stir till it leaves the sides of the pan. When thick, spread it on a board and cut into slices while still warm. Store in tins.

coconut biscuits

Anglo-Indian, Mertel Gomez

A tasty snack, the sweetness is reduced when served with tea

Maida / All purpose flour ~ 2 kg
Sugar ~ 2 kg
Butter/ Dalda ~ 2 kg
Nutmeg ~ 1
Baking powder ~ 1 tsp
Coconuts ~ 8, grated

Cream sugar and butter / dalda together till creamy. Add the flour and mix well. To this, add nutmeg and the grated coconut.

Make into balls, flatten and bake at 175°c in a pre-heated oven. Cool and store in tins.

soulinh

Anglo-Indian, Mertel Gomez

Coconut oil is the popular fat used in Kerala. Substitute this with vegetable oil, if desired

Rice flour ~ 2 cups
Egg ~ 1
Maida or all purpose flour ~ ½ cup
Kerala plantains ~ 3, mashed to a lumpy pulp
Coconut milk ~ 1 cup, first milk
Jaggery ~ ¾ cup
Salt ~ 1 pinch
Cardamom powder ~ ½ tsp
Coconut oil ~ 2 cups

Heat jaggery in a pan over low flame till the syrup melts. Take off the fire and add the coconut milk, rice flour, flour, egg, salt and the pulped plantain.

Mix all the ingredients together and knead well. Then keep aside for two hours.

Heat oil in a round-bottomed pan. Transfer scoops of the mixture into boiling oil using a deep spoon. Deep fry till golden brown.

bebinca

Anglo-Indian, Faylene Lobo

Different from the Bebinca made in Goa, this one uses Kerala plantain and whole eggs to form a cake like preparation

Boiled rice flour ~ ½ kg
Kerala bananas, ripe and steamed ~ 10
Eggs ~ 5
Sugar ~ 10 tbsp
Salted butter ~ ¼ kg
Nutmeg, grated ~ 2
Coconut milk ~ 1½ coconuts, first and second milk

Make coconut milk (with 1½ cups of water for the first milk and two cups of water for the second milk). Heat the milks separately and keep aside to cool.

Mix chopped banana and eggs in a mixing bowl and add the butter, rice flour, sugar, nutmeg and first milk. Use the second milk to turn the mixture into a pouring batter consistency. Grease and flour a cake tin and bake the mixture for 45 minutes at 180°c or till cooked. Serve sliced.

cha cha

Anglo-Indian, Faylene Lobo

Cha cha is a snack customarily made as children's evening snack when they return from school. Ingredients are similar to the cha cha of the Malabari Jews; however the cooking process changes the sweetmeat altogether

Coconut ~ 1, thick milk
Cardamom ~ 5
Sugar ~ ½ cup
Kerala banana, ripe and sliced round ~ 2
Rice flour ~ ¼ kg
Hot water as required
Salt ~ to taste

Make coconut milk using five cups of water and heat the milk with the cardamom and sugar over a low flame until steam rises.

Mix the remaining ingredients using hot water to form a soft ball of dough. Make small balls from it, flattening it between the thumb and index fingers (keeping two aside for later use).

Drop these into the coconut milk along with the sliced bananas. Make a paste with the two remaining balls and add it to the milk to thicken.

bole coke

Anglo-Indian, Faylene Lobo

Faylene recommends the addition of an extra 100 gm of butter to obtain a richer, finer texture

Broiled rava / sooji ~ ½ kg
Sugar ~ ¼ to ½ kg, based on required sweetness
Ghee ~ 250 gm
Eggs ~ 10, separated
Cardamom ~ 8, ground
Coconuts ~ 2, ground in rose water

Make a thick syrup of sugar and cool. Add the rava, ghee, egg yolks, ground coconut and cardamom.

Beat the egg white till stiff and fold into the mixture.

Grease and flour a cake tin and bake the mixture at 180°c for 45 minutes or till done.

layered pancake in syrup

Anglo-Indian, Faylene Lobo

The limejuice gives a tangy feel to an otherwise sweet dessert. Lime can be replaced with orange juice for a completely new flavour (reduce sugar as required)

Maida or all-purpose flour ~ 2 cups
Eggs ~ 2, beaten
Milk ~ ½ cup or to make a thin batter
Sugar ~ 3 tbsp
Water ~ ¾ cup
Limejuice ~ ½ to 1 lime

Dissolve the sugar in water and heat over a low flame to make thick syrup. When cool, add the limejuice and keep aside.

Beat the rest of the ingredients together to form a semi-thick batter.

Heat a pan and pour a ladle of batter to make even sized pancakes. Cook each pancake to a golden brown, turning it when required.

Layer each of the pancakes with the sugar syrup, placing them one over the other. Serve warm.

chakkara choru

SWEET RICE

Malabar Mappila, Rasheeda and Rahima Meethalakath

Choru refers to rice and Rasheeda and Rahima also substitute this recipe with sugar, for a change of flavour. Sometimes broken wheat is used instead of rice. Chakkara choru is also eaten in Christian homes. My mother recalls it as a high-energy snack her mother served after a tired day at school

White rice ~ 1 cup
Coconut milk ~ first and second milk of one coconut
Melted jiggery ~ 1 cup
Cardamom powder ~ a pinch
Salt ~ a pinch
Water ~ to cook rice

Cook the rice to a three quarter consistency along with the salt. Add the second coconut milk and cook again.

Add the melted jaggery and the cardamom powder.

Once the rice is done and the liquid is almost dry, add the first coconut milk and let it boil once. Switch off after the boil.

This dessert can be served warm or at room temperature.

van payar paysam

RED GRAM RICE PUDDING (PAIYSAM)

Malabar Mappila, Rasheeda and Rahima Meethalakath

This sweetmeat is a Malabari variation of the paiysam (payasam) prepared in various parts of Kerala and is best when served warm. Another version of the paiysam is to use grated coconut and raggi instead of rice powder

Rice powder ~ 2 tbsp
Red gram ~ 1 cup
Melted jaggery ~ 250 gm
Cardamom powder ~ ½ tsp
Rice powder ~ ½ cup
Coconut milk ~ first and second milk of one coconut
Salt ~ A pinch
Water ~ Enough to cover the gram

Cook the red gram in water and salt. Add the rice powder to the second milk and mix thoroughly. Now add the jaggery, red beans and let it boil.

After the first boil, add the first milk and the cardamom powder and allow it to boil once again.

Remove the vessel from the fire.

kozhalappam vailiyachathu

CARAMELISED KOZHALAPPAM

Syrian Christian, Sara Mamen and Marie Geevarghese

The process of coating kozhalappam with jaggery is referred to as vailiyachathu. The marrying of sesame seeds, cumin, and jaggery gives an interesting flavour. The addition of shallots is for an acquired taste

Rice powder ~ 6 cups
Shallots ~ ¾ cups
Coconut ~ 3½ cups, grated
Black sesame seeds ~ 1 tbsp
Cumin seeds ~ 1 tbsp
Salt ~ to taste
Water ~ 2-3 cups; 1½ cups
Oil ~ for frying
Jaggery ~ 250 gm

Grind the cumin seeds, shallots and black sesame seeds. Boil the water and add the salt to it. Heat the rice powder slightly in a large pan and add the coconut to it. Once the coconut dries, add the hot water and mix well. Add ground mixture along with the sesame seeds.

Make balls the size of a gooseberry and roll them out to form flat bread-like shapes. Wrap this around the handle of a wooden spoon to get a hollow cylinder.

Heat the oil and fry till golden brown.

for the sweet coating

Make syrup by heating the jaggery with 1½ cups of water. Allow it to cool and add the fried kozhalappam to it. Allow them to coat with the syrup. Store in an airtight container when cool.

thenga velliacha pancake

KERALA COCONUT CREPES

Latin Catholic, Annie Burleigh Kurishingal

A very popular dessert or snack in Kerala, the filling can change in flavour with the addition or omission of spices like cardamom. Raisins and cashews are also added, but remain optional. This sweetmeat cannot be necessarily assigned to a particular community alone, although mostly made in Kerala Christian homes

for the filling

Coconut ~ 1 cup, grated

Jaggery ~ ½ cup

Cardamom (optional) ~ ½ tsp powder

Water to moisten the filling

Dissolve the jaggery in water and strain it. Place it on the fire over medium to low heat. When it thickens, add the coconut. Stir till it becomes dry but remains moist and soft. Add the cardamom powder and mix well. Remove from fire.

for the batter

Flour ~ 1 cup
Eggs ~ 2
Milk ~ ½ cup
Water ~ 2-3 tbsp
Salt ~ ¼ tsp salt
Butter ~ 2 tbsp, melted

Whisk the eggs well. To it, add the flour, milk and water alternatively, whisking well to make a fine batter without any lumps. Add the salt and beat well.

Heat a frying pan on medium heat and run it with melted butter.

Pour a ladleful of batter and tilt the pan till it covers the bottom evenly. Cook for 2 minutes. Turn it with a spatula and cook a minute more.

Overturn it on a plate. Place the filling on one side of the crepe and roll it. Serve hot.

bread caramel pudding

Anglo-Indian, Faylene Lobo

Popular in Christian homes, this is a version of the caramel custard, which is usually made from a day old bread

Bread ~ 8-10 slices
Eggs ~ 3
Sugar ~ 1 cup
Milk ~ 3 cups
Butter ~ To spread on bread

Butter the bread slices and keep aside.

Beat the eggs along with ½-¾ cups of sugar (depending on the sweetness required). Add milk and mix well. Make a caramel of the remaining sugar by heating it in a heavy bottom pan on very low heat or on a double boiler.

Stir occasionally to ensure it does not burn. Once it changes colour to a golden brown, remove from the fire and pour into a baking dish. Arrange the bread slices over the caramel and pour the milk mixture on it, ensuring the bread slices are all soaked well.

Steam for 20 minutes, or till the pudding is cooked.

karikku pudding

TENDER COCONUT PUDDING

Syrian Christian, Sarala Thomas Pallivathukal

A later-day dessert, the original recipe calls for milk to be boiled for long hours to a condensed form. With the availability of condensed milk, the laborious process of cooking milk has been eliminated. Condensed milk was considered a 'god-sent' ingredient that came to be used in a number of desserts in homes across Kerala. Such was the popularity that for the longest time it was known in Kerala homes by the only brand available in India, Milk Maid

Tender coconuts ~ 8, flesh
Coconut water ~ 1½ cups
China grass ~ 75 gm
Condensed milk ~ 1 tin
Milk ~ 2 tins (use the tin of condensed milk)
Water ~ 1 cup

Soak china grass in water for three hours. Now, over low heat, melt it. Add the coconut water and when it warms, add the milk and condensed milk stirring well.

When it begins to thicken, remove from the fire and allow it to cool. Add the tender coconut flesh and mix.

Pour into a dish and chill till set.

kozhukkattai

STEAMED RICE DUMPLINGS WITH COCONUT

Syrian Christian, Mary Mathew Madathikunnel

Made largely by the Christians of Kerala, it is a 'must' snack on Kozhukkatta Saturday, the day before Palm Sunday and the 41st day of Lent. Koozhukkatai is usually had as a snack at teatime

Rice flour ~ 1 cup
Coconut ~ 1½ cups, shredded
Jaggery ~ ½ cup, made from boiling jaggery pieces in water
Water ~ 1 cup
Salt ~ a pinch
Oil ~ to moisten the palms

Boil the water with the oil and salt. Pour it into the rice powder, mixing it well in the process till a firm dough is formed. Roast the coconut for a few minutes over low flame, add the sieved jaggery syrup to it and cook till the coconut is well coated.

Moisten palms with some oil and make balls of the dough, about the size of a small egg.

Make a deep depression in each ball and spoon the coconut mixture into them. Seal the sides of the balls and steam till the dough is cooked.

madura cheeda

Syrian Christian, Mary Mathew Madathikunnel

Cheeda is a popular snack made by Christians during Christmas time. This snack is usually made a month in advance and stored in air-tight containers. It has a good shelf life

Rice flour ~ 1½ cups, roasted
Coconut ~ ¾ cup, grated
Sugar ~ 1 cup
Cumin ~ ½ tsp
Water ~ 1 cup
Salt ~ to taste
Oil ~ for frying

In a pan, roast the coconut until all the water evaporates. Grind and keep aside.

Make dough by mixing the rice powder with the ground coconut, cumin, salt and sufficient water. Make small balls and slightly flatten with the fingers to two inches length. Use a fork and make impressions on these, folding them inward so that the marks are visible.

Heat the water and add the sugar to make medium-thick syrup. Heat the oil and fry the flattened balls till golden brown. Place them on an absorbent paper till excess oil leaves the cheeda.

Dip them in the sugar syrup for a few minutes and remove. The sugar will form a coating on the cheeda, making it sweet.

sukian

Malabari Jews, Ilanit Menachem

This is a snack usually eaten during teatime and found throughout Kerala. Sukian is popularly made in Christian and Jewish homes. Ilanit Menachem has shared this recipe, which was handed down by her mother

1. Green lentils ~ 1 cup, soaked for a few hours
   Sugar ~ 1½ cups
   Coconut ~ 1 cup, shredded
   Cardamom ~ 4, ground
   Salt ~ A pinch
   Water ~ 2 cups
2. Flour ~ 1 cup
   Rice flour ~ 2 tbsp
   Coconut milk ~ ½ cup
   Oil ~ 3 tbsp

Boil and cook the lentils in water till soft. Add the coconut, sugar, and the salt and cook over low heat. Once it begins to boil, add the cardamom and continue cooking on medium heat till all the water evaporates. Allow the filling mixture to cool.

In the meantime, make a batter for coating the balls and frying them by mixing all the ingredients in 2 together. The consistency must be thick to coat the balls well; thus add the coconut milk as required to attain that thickness.

Make small balls of the filling, dip in the batter and drop them one at a time in hot oil to fry them.

Remove when golden brown and serve warm or cool.

undah madrom

SEMOLINA BALLS IN SWEET COCONUT SAUCE

Malabari Jews, Ilanit Menachem

1. Semolina ~ 1 cup
   Rice ~ ¼ cup, ground fine in a blender to form a powder
   Coconut ~ ½ cup, shredded
   Flour ~ ½ cup
   Oil ~ ¼ cup
   Salt ~ a pinch
2. Coconut milk ~ 2 cups
   Sugar ~ 1½ cups
   Cardamom ~ 1-2 pinches, ground
   Water ~ 4 cups
   Salt ~ a small pinch

Boil the water along with the sugar, salt and oil. Mix the ingredients in 1 to make the dough. Make balls of the dough and drop them in the boiling water. Cook till the balls begin to float.

Now add the coconut milk and the cardamom and stir gently lest the balls break. Allow it to boil, then lower the heat and let it boil for another five minutes.

Allow it to cool and refrigerate. Serve cold.

saori

TAPIOCA IN COCONUT CREAM

Malabari Jews, Ilanit Menachem

This recipe is also found in Christian homes, where tapioca is substituted with bread fruit. The cooking process is long because of the time tapioca takes to cook. An option is to par-cook it in a pressure cooker and add the pieces to the sugar-water

Sugar ~ 2 cups
Tapioca ~ 1½ cups
Coconut milk ~ 3 cups, first milk
Cardamom powder ~ 2 pinches
Salt ~ a pinch

Boil the water with sugar. Add the tapioca when the water boils and allow it to cook till soft. When done, add the coconut milk, cardamom and the salt. Stir constantly, breaking any lumps formed of the tapioca with a spoon. Serve hot or cold.

atz'afom /achappam

ROSE COOKIES

Malabari Jews, Ilanit Menachem

A very popular snack in Kerala. Believed to have been of Dutch influence, the recipe is simple but requires a mould. Latin Catholics, Syrian Christians, Anglo-Indians and Jews make this snack known under different names—Rose cookies for the Anglo-Indians, Atz'afom for the Jews and Achappam for the rest. Christians add black sesame seed to the batter, whilst the Jews prefer cardamom

Flour ~ 1 cup
Eggs ~ 2 cups
Sugar ~ ½ cup
Water ~ as required
Salt ~ a pinch
Oil ~ for frying

Heat sufficient oil in a deep pan. Beat the eggs and add the flour, sugar and salt, mixing while slowly pouring the water into it.

When mixed well and attained a semi-thick consistency, dip the mould into the hot oil and then dip it into the batter. The batter will stick to the mould.

Now transfer the mould into the oil and gently shake the batter off the mould. This process requires skill and calls for some practice before the perfect achappam is made.

falt'zori

RICE BALLS IN COCONUT

Malabari Jews, Ilanit Menachem

The ingredients are similar to the Anglo-Indian Cha cha (except for the banana).The cooking process changes the flavour and consistency

Rice powder ~ 1cup, roasted
Coconut ~ 1 cup, shredded
Cardamom ~ 4, ground
Sugar ~ 1½ cups
Salt ~ A pinch
Water ~ 3 cups

Boil water with the sugar and salt. Once it begins to boil, add the coconut and cardamom and stir. Now add the rice powder and cook on low heat till the mixture thickens. Let it cool then chill it. Make small balls with the palm of your hands.

jewish banana cake

Malabari Jews, Ilanit Menachem

Cardamom is an optional ingredient, used mostly by the Jews. Ilanit recalls this cake being made by her grandmother in a pot, once she moved from Cochin to Israel. Later it was baked in an indigenous oven

Semolina ~ 1 cup
Sugar ~ 1¼ cups
Oil ~ ¼ cup
Flour ~ 2 cups
Water ~ ½ cup
Bananas ~ 6, diced
Cardamom ~ 2 tsp, powdered

Mix all the dry ingredients together. Add the banana and continue mixing. The mixture can be grilled in a flat pan to get bread or in an oven for cake.

The cake is done when the top browns and the insides are baked, which one checks by inserting a toothpick.

The banana bread the Christians make follows a similar recipe but instead of semolina, only rice flour is used.

coconut crepes

(PHOTO ON P.163)

Latin Catholic, Annie Burleigh Kurishingal

Also referred to as Kerala pancakes, jaggery can be replaced with sugar

for the batter

Flour ~ 1 cup

Eggs (optional) ~ 1, beaten

Milk or water ~ As required to make a thin batter

Salt ~ A pinch

for the filling

Shredded coconut ~ 2 cups

Dark jaggery syrup ~ ½ cup

Cardamom powder (optional) ~ A pinch

Cook the coconut with the jaggery syrup over low heat until the coconut is soaked in it. (Ensure that the consistency is a moist one; avoid overcooking it.)

Make the batter with the ingredients mentioned, make flat crepes on a heated girdle.

Stuff them with two tablespoonfuls of the filling and roll tightly.

SQUASHES AND WINES
(with a dash of spice)

bilimbipuli squash

GREEN TAMARIND SQUASH

Syrian Christian, Mary Mathew Madathikunnel

Bilimbipuli – ½ kg
Sugar – 1 kg
Water – 2 cups
Limejuice – optional and as required

Beat the bilimbi in a mixer with ¼ cup water. Strain well and keep the juice aside.

Boil the remaining water along with the sugar in a vessel. When the sugar is dissolved, remove the pot from the fire and add the strained juice. Add limejuice to increase the tartness, if required.

Pour into dry, clean and airtight bottles and refrigerate.

Serve adding water as needed and chill the drink with ice cubes if required.

tamarind juice

Latin Christian, Annie Burleigh Kurishingal

A perfect summer drink, my grandmother used to add a dash of turmeric powder for its healthy properties

Tamarind – A palmful, shell removed
Water – 5-7 cups, to dilute the juice as required
Sugar – to taste
Cinnamon – 2 sticks, one inch long

~

Boil the water and soak the tamarind in it for half an hour.

Add the sugar and stir till well dissolved. Strain the liquid, add the cinnamon sticks and chill in the fridge.

tender coconut and coconut milk drink

Syrian Christian, Sarala Thomas Pallivathukkal

Coconut – ½ cup, first milk
Tender coconut – 1, water and pulp
Sugar – As required and based on the sweetness of the tender coconut
Mint leaves – to garnish

~

Mix the ingredients well, beating till it is frothy. Chill.

Garnish with mint leaves and serve.

wine with fresh grapes

WINDOW TO WINES

Both Jews and Christians of Kerala have the tradition of making wines. Both traditions come from similar backgrounds, grapes signifying the fruit of the earth. Although Christians largely make wine to celebrate Christmas, New Year and Easter; Cochinni Jews have a ready stock of it at all times for the celebration of Passover. The difference between the two, however, lies in Jews avoiding yeast in their wine, following the tradition of their ancestors ("... And you shall observe the Feast of Unleavened Bread, for on this very day I brought your hosts out of the land of Egypt. Therefore you shall observe this day, throughout your generations, as a statute forever. In the first month, from the fourteenth day of the month at evening, you shall eat unleavened bread until the twenty-first day of the month at evening: Exodus 12: 17, 18 ESV version"). Christians' use of fermented wine signifies the coming of Christ through whom all traditions and laws are seen as man-made.

Paradesi Jew, Sarah Cohen

Black grapes ~ 10 kg
Sugar ~ 5 kg

Wash and destalk the grapes. Allow the water to drain from it for an hour.

In a big jar, alternate the grapes with sugar till the top. Close the jar with its lid. Stir the grapes and the sugar daily with a long wooden spoon.

By the 15th day, the sugar would have melted. Decant the mixture by pouring into a large colander, allowing the liquid to be collected in a vessel placed below it.

Place an unbreakable plate or lid on the grapes upon which weights are placed so that all the liquid drains out. Allow the process to take place for a few hours.

Pour the wine into clean bottles and store.

wine with dry grapes or raisins

Paradesi Jew, Sarah Cohen

Raisins ~ 10 kg
Water ~ to cover the raisins

Wash the raisins well and place them in a large vessel. Pour enough water to cover the raisins (water and raisins must remain at the same level).

Keep the vessel covered by tying it with a cloth tightly at its mouth. Mix the raisins daily, stirring from bottom upwards.

On the fifth day, mince the raisins in a blender. Place the minced raisins and its juice back into the vessel. Continue turning the pulp every day, for the next eight days.

On the eighth day, pour out the wine and throw away the residue.

Bottle the wine and store.

pineapple squash

Paradesi Jew, Queenie Hallegua

Pineapple ~ 2, ripe and blended to a puree
Water ~ 1 litre
Sugar ~ 1.5 kg-2 kg, as per the sweetness required
Citric acid ~ 30 gm

Mix all the ingredients one by one in a wok on fire and cook till the squash is thick in consistency and the sugar and citric acid are well dissolved and blended.

Take off the fire, cool it and preserve in a refrigerator, stored in a dry and clean bottle as the concentrate. Add cold water and ice cubes to serve as a squash drink.

TIMELINE

Arrival of St Thomas Christians – AD 52

Arrival of Arabs – 7th century AD

Arrival of Malabari Jews (documented evidence) – 10th century AD, first reference 10th century BC

Arrival of Paradesi Jews – 16th century AD

Arrival of the Portuguese and Catholicism – 16th century AD

Departure of Jews to the new state of Israel – 1950 onwards

GLOSSARY OF SPICES

Cardamom, *elakka* - used whole or ground
Cinnamon, *patta* - used as whole sticks or ground
Clove, *grambu* - used whole or ground
Coriander, *mallli* - used whole or ground, also fresh leaves
Cocum, *kodumpulli* - used in its dry form
Tamarind, *valanpuli* - whole, ground/paste
Cumin, *Jeerakam* - used whole or ground
Curry leaves, *Karivepala*

Used fresh

Garlic, *velutha ulli* - used whole, sliced, paste, dry powder
Ginger, *inchi* - sliced, ground/paste
Fenugreek, *uluva* - used as seeds, leaves
Pepper, *kurumolagu* - used whole, crushed and as powder
Tamarind, *eramban/bilimbipuli* - whole/sliced
Nutmeg, *jadhikka* - used ground/powdered
Mustard, *kadugu* - used whole, ground/paste

Used powdered

Turmeric, *manjal* - used as powder, paste
Red chilli powder - *mullagu podi*
Turmeric powder - *manjal podi*
Coriander powder - *malli podi*
Garam masala powder - *masala podi*

TRADITIONAL COOKING TOOLS (IN KERALA KITCHENS)

Kudam: Pot with lid, used to cook rice, boil water etc.

Arakalu: Used to grind or paste spices, coconut etc.

Uruli: Large urns used for cooking, made of brass.

Uralu: Used to powder grain. A granite base with a heavy wooden pounder (pestle). The pestle had an iron cup on one end and a ring on the other. The end with ring was used to chaff grain and the other to powder.

Cheenachatti: Wok, brought to Kerala by the Chinese (*Cheena* refers to China), usually in cast iron.

Mannchatti: Vessels made of baked clay. These are made for specific uses. For example, *meenchatti* is used to make fish curry (*meen* means fish).

Bharani: Urns, ceramic or clay. Traditional *bharani* came from China, used to bring products of trade down the Spice Route.

Puttu kodum, Puttu kuti: Utensils used to make *puttu. The kuti* was originally made of bamboo or coconut shell.

Appachatti: Used to make *vellaiappam,* made of cast iron.

kerala garam masala powder recipe

Cardamom ~ 4
Cloves ~ 10
Cinnamon stick ~ 1", 2 pieces
Fennel seeds ~ 1 tsp
Star anise ~ 1 piece

Dry roast the spices and powder to a fine consistency.
A mix of various spices, this spice mix takes the place of individual spices to flavour a dish, largely used in meat preparations.

TABLE OF MEASURES

In all recipes imperial equivalents of metric measures are shown in parentheses e.g. 1lb (500 gm) lamb. Although the metric yields of cup and weighed measures are approximately 10% greater that the imperial yields, the proportions remain the same. Therefore for successful cooking use either metric or imperial weights or measures—do not mix the two.

Imperial Weight	**Metric Weight**
½ oz	15 gm
1 oz	30 gm
2 oz	60 gm
3 oz	90 gm
4 oz (¼ lb)	152 gm
6 oz	185 gm
8 oz (½ lb)	250 gm
12 oz (¾ lb)	375 gm
16 oz (1lb)	500 gm
24 oz (1½ lb)	750 gm
32 oz (2 lb)	1000 gm (1kg)
3 lb	1500 gm (1½ kg)
4 lb	2000 gm (2 kg)
oz = ounce, gm = gram, lb = pound, kg = kilogram	

Imperial Liquid Measures	**Cup Measures**	**Metric Liquid Measures**
1 fl oz		30 ml
2 fl oz	¼ cup	60 ml
3 fl oz		100 ml
4 fl oz	½ cup	140 ml
5 fl oz	¾ cup	150 ml
6 fl oz	1cup	
8 fl oz	1¼ cups	250 ml

10 fl oz	1½ cups	
12 fl oz	1¾ cups	
14 fl oz	2 cups	
16 fl oz	2½ cups	500 ml
fl = fluid ounce, ml = mililitre		

OVEN TEMPERATURE GUIDE

Oven description	Celsius (°c)	Fahrenheit (°F)	Gas Mark
Cool	100	200	¼
Very slow	120	250	½
Slow	150	300	2
Moderately slow	160	325	3
Moderate	180	350	4
Moderately hot	190	375	5
Hot	200	400	6
Very hot	230	450	8

ACKNOWLEDGEMENTS

To Therasachedathi, for her toil in the kitchen to serve us delicious fare learnt from my grandmother, from the time ammama could cook no more for her failing health.
To the recipe contributors: Anglo Indian - Mertel Gomez, Fort Kochi; Faylene Lobo, Vypeen; Hilda Rodrigues, Ernakulam; Howard La'frenais, Fort Kochi.
Latin Catholic - From the recipe books of Late Annie Burleigh Kurishingal; Preea Kurishingal Mathai, Fort Kochi; Sophy Thomas Kurishingal, Fort Kochi; Pearl Prakash Kurishingal, Fort Kochi.
Syrian Christian - (*For convenience's sake, no distinction is made here between Syrian* Catholic and Syrian Christian) Rema Tharakan. Recipes from the Parayil family; Sara Mamen and Marie Geevarghese. Recipes from the Ikareth family; Sarala Thomas Pallivathukal, Kottayam. Recipes from Kootiparambil and Parayil families; Sheelu Thomas. Recipes from Thresiama Eapen Kadamapuzha, Kanjirapally; Sophy Thomas Kurishingal aka Mathew Madathikunnel. Recipes from Mary Mathew Madathikunnel, Pala.
Cochin Jews - Ilanit Menachem. Jerusalem, Israel (Paravaur Jew descendant); Quennie Hallegua and Late Sarah Cohen, Jew Town, Mattancherry.
Malabar Muslim, also referred to as Mappila - Rasheed and Rahima Meethalakath, Thalassery. Recipes from family recipe books handed down generations, Razia Hafiz Acharath Parakkat Mahal
Others - KR Sunil, Mythri Babu for the photographs; Chef Biju and Chef R. Vibhin and the team of Old Harbour Hotel, Fort Kochi for support in food photography; Dr Midhun C Sekhar for the ancient Dutch map on the back cover; Edgar Pinto for the title; Priti Vadakkath for sharing her drawing of Kurishingal Tarawad; Mathrubhumi for photographs of the Malabar Muslim community; Tirza Lavi, Meydad Eliyahu, Meir Nehemia, Late Sarah Cohen and Muziris Heritage Project for photographs of the Jewish communities; Kurishingal family for images from their family albums; Eapen Thomas for images of Kadamapuzha family, Syrian Christian.
Praveen Rengaraj, Shibin Balakrishnan for photography; Craig and Dennis D'Costa for photos, Anglo-Indian; Unsplash, for use of images. Sunny Malayil of Crafters, Jew Town for lending antique crockery for the recipe shoot.

Many thanks to my editor, Mohua Mitra (Niyogi Books), for her support and feedback. It was such pleasure working with her. Thanks to the designer, Nabanita Das (Niyogi Books), for her work in making the book visually luring.

'Thank you' and gratitude to the publishers Bikash and Tultul Niyogi, and to Nirmalkanti Bhattacharjee for lending publishing support, having faith in my work and understanding the importance of preserving history, which is vivid in ancient culinary food, for the generations to come.

Other food and cuisine books from
the Niyogi Books stable that you may like to read